Accounting for Infrastructure Regulation

Accounting for Infrastructure Regulation

An Introduction

Martin Rodriguez Pardina

Richard Schlirf Rapti

Eric Groom

THE WORLD BANK
Washington, DC

ISBN: 978-0-8213-7179-4
eISBN: 978-0-8213-7180-0
DOI: 10.1596/ 978-0-8213-7179-4

Library of Congress Cataloging-in-Publication Data

Rodríguez Pardina, Martin, 1961–
    Accounting for infrastructure regulation : an introduction / Martin Rodríguez Pardina, Richard Schlirf Rapti, Eric Groom.
    p. cm.
    Includes bibliographical references and index.
    ISBN-13: 978-0-8213-7179-4
    ISBN-10: 0-8213-7179-7
    ISBN-10: 0-8213-7180-0 (electronic)
    1. Infrastructure (Economics)—Government policy.   2. Infrastructure (Economics)—Government policy.   3. Public utilities—Accounting—Government policy.   4. Corporations—Accounting—Government policy.   5. Disclosure in accounting—Government policy.
I. Rapti, Richard Schlirf, 1960–   II. Groom, Eric, 1954–   III. Title.
HC79.c3r63 2007
657'.838—dc22

                                                                                    2007017934

Contents

Foreword

The Enron crisis offered a dramatic reminder to regulators around the world that reliable accounting standards are essential for markets to work efficiently and fairly. Harvey Pitt, chairman of the regulatory agency responsible for the monitoring of accountants in the United States (the Securities and Exchange Commission) from 2001 to 2003, argued that the crisis revealed two problems with accounting that needed to be addressed by the regulators. The first problem is that the accountants may have gotten some of the accounting wrong. The second, and more important, problem is that they may have gotten a lot of the accounting right (see http://www.pbs.org/wgbh/pages/frontline/shows/regulation/lessons/).

This general point should ring true to anyone working on utilities regulation. For utilities, as for any other sector, poor accounting practice or creative accounting generates winners and losers. Whoever controls the accounting information is likely to be the winner; the others—including the users, who will pay excessive tariffs, or the taxpayers, who will be asked to justify unjustified subsidies—will be the losers. Failure to recognize this reality figures prominently in many of the high-profile conflicts from Latin America to Africa over distribution of the rents created by reform processes.

In the future, utilities regulators will need to be much more serious about ensuring that accounting rules are spelled out. Clear rules are essential to the implementation of the regulatory designs intended to achieve a fair distribution of operational gains and losses among all actors. In many countries in crisis, such a distribution is likely to help investors and operators as much as taxpayers and users, because it will tend to generate the information needed for accurate estimation of returns to businesses.

To ensure that this information is generated without penalizing anyone, regulatory accounting rules must be explicit. This volume describes a set of rules with which utilities monopolies should be able to comply without threat to a fair return on their business, while at the same time ensuring the accountability of all players. Regulators in many member countries of the Organisation for Economic Co-operation and Development and in the electricity sector in many developing countries use these rules. There is no reason why they should not be of value to regulators of all public service providers that enjoy strong residual monopoly rights. Ultimately, this book is about rules for maintaining the minimum level of accountability needed to achieve fair treatment of investors, operators, users, and taxpayers alike and to prevent preferential treatment of the stakeholder with the highest political leverage at any point in time.

Antonio Estache
Senior Economic Adviser
Sustainable Development Network
The World Bank

Acknowledgments

This volume draws on the knowledge of many regulators and utilities analysts around the world. Some of these experts are colleagues; others have provided work that we have used without benefit of collaboration. Regulatory accounting is a burgeoning field of endeavor, and regulators are increasingly establishing and publishing regulatory accounting requirements and standards. Awareness of and reference to all these efforts is impossible. Our apologies go to those we have neither cited nor sourced.

We owe a special thanks to Commissioner Rauf Tan (Energy Regulatory Commission of the Philippines) and Fiona Towers (Independent Pricing and Regulatory Tribunal of New South Wales, Australia) for their careful review of and insightful comments on the draft of this volume. We would also thank Anwar Ravat, Sergio Perelman, Lourdes Trujillo, Charles Kenny, Tony Gomez-Ibanez, Daniel Benitez and Tina Soreide for useful and perceptive comments and discussions, and the many World Bank staff members who participated in workshops related to the volume and who provided valuable guidance.

Special thanks also go to Tomas Serebrisky, who, with support from Antonio Estache and Clive Harris, managed the project from which this volume emerged.

Finally, we wish to acknowledge the World Bank Infrastructure Economics and Finance Department and the World Bank Institute for support and funding.

Abbreviations

ABC	activity-based costing [cost-allocation method]
AFUDC	allowance for funds used during construction
AGL	Australian Gas Light Company
FDC	fully distributed cost [accounting approach to cost allocation]
FRS	financial reporting standard
GAAP	generally accepted accounting principles
IASB	International Accounting Standards Board
ICC	Interstate Commerce Commission [U.S.]
IFRS	International Financial Reporting Standards
IPART	Independent Pricing and Regulatory Tribunal (New South Wales)
IV	indicative value
MAR	market-to-asset ratio
MMC	Monopolies and Mergers Commission (United Kingdom)
NER	National Electricity Regulator (South Africa)
PCG	Plan Comptable Général
RAGs	regulatory accounting guidelines
RPI-X	retail price index minus expected future productivity gains
Syscoa	Système Comptable Ouest-Africain

Why Accounting Information Matters

In the last 20 or so years, infrastructure sectors all over the world have undergone a deep transformation. Starting with deregulation in the United States and deregulation and privatization in the United Kingdom, the movement quickly spread to other countries, notably countries in Latin America but also those in Africa and Asia.

In many cases the restructuring involved the introduction of competition in the market in at least some service segments. Among these segments were long-distance calls in the telecommunications sector, and production and supply in energy markets (electricity and gas).

But competition was not a possibility in sectors characterized by large sunk investments, a large share of fixed costs, and economies of scale and scope. In these sectors the efficient economic decision is to have just one service provider, which means that regulation was necessarily an integral part of the transformation.

A key element in the transformation of activities in which competition was not a solution was the division of policy-making, regulator, and service-provider functions into distinct institutions. In the past, many state-owned enterprises had been performing—legally or de facto—all three functions, but the reform wave of the 1990s stressed the need to move regulation into an independent body. In many cases the transformation also involved the participation of the private sector in provision of the service.

Economic theory suggests that a monopolist will have strong incentives to reduce quantities and raise prices, reducing total welfare in society.[1] The solution to this market failure is to impose certain restrictions on the behavior of the firm through direct or indirect regulation of profits, prices, and service conditions.

Although natural monopolies have been regulated for well over a century, not until the late 1970s and early 1980s did economic theory consider information to be a key element of the regulatory game. Laffont (1999) points out two important theoretical milestones. First, Loeb and Magat (1979) propose viewing regulation as a contractual relationship in which a regulator, the principal, attempts to control a firm, the agent. They emphasize that the main difficulty is the regulator's lack of information about the regulated firm. Second, Baron and Myerson (1982) show that there is a trade-off between efficiency and the unavoidable informational rents that must be given up to a regulated firm when the regulator wants a project to be realized but does not know the cost of the regulated firm.

Since these seminal studies appeared, economists have understood regulation as a game of two players—the regulator and the firm—that do not share the same information. Laffont and Tirole's (1994) model with cost or profit observability and with asymmetry of information about the firm's technology and (unobservable) cost-reducing efforts became the basic paradigm of the theoretical analysis of regulation.

While economic theory moved toward highlighting the role of information in regulation, regulatory practice in many countries appeared to move in the opposite direction. The introduction of price-cap regulation in the United Kingdom with the RPI-X (retail price index minus expected future productivity gains) system was interpreted—erroneously—by many practitioners as a mechanism that freed them from the need to rely on detailed information on regulated companies. With the regulatory function limited to estimating the efficiency factor once every four or five years, there appeared to be little need to generate a detailed system of information on the regulated firm or firms.[2]

After 10 years of regulatory practice in the wake of many countries' restructuring of infrastructure sectors in the 1990s, this false perception is rapidly vanishing, and the unavoidable need for a reliable information system that enables regulators to fulfill their complex objectives has become even clearer. As Estache and Burns (1999a, 1) point out,

> [t]he initial ineffectiveness of regulation resulting from information gaps creates allocative inefficiencies but just as important carries political and social ramifications which can endanger the stability of the regulatory regime. In developing countries, this influences the incentives to operate efficiently and the cost of investment and often ends up threatening the sustainability of the increased role of the private sector in the delivery of infrastructure services and ultimately, the foundations of the overall reform process itself.

This context is one in which a regulatory accounting system is an important source of reliable information for regulators to use to adequately fulfill their duties.

Good, accurate, and consistent information provides the basis of effective regulation. Regulatory accounting can help to establish a reasonably defined and stable reporting regime. As Byatt (1991, 124) points out,

> *stability in the reporting cycle and avoidance of ad hoc requests should assist those planning and managing the industry. It should also facilitate the integration of information systems for both internal and external reporting.*

Chapter 1 of this volume sets up the conceptual framework of regulation. It discusses the main regulatory objectives and the information needs derived from them. Chapter 2 presents three case studies illustrating some of the typical informational problems faced by regulators all over the world.

Chapters 3 and 4 cover the main elements of standard management information systems and statutory and cost accounting. The objective is to introduce the main accounting principles and concepts for those who are not familiar with them. Those who have a working understanding of these topics can skip these chapters without losing the thread of the discussion.

Chapter 5 presents the main elements of regulatory accounting, stressing similarities to and differences with statutory and cost accounting principles. Chapter 6 covers in some detail four of the main elements of regulatory accounting: separation of activities, the regulatory asset base, depreciation policies of the regulatory asset base, and transactions with related parties. Chapter 7 presents an outline of regulatory accounting guidelines.

1.1. Objectives of public service regulation

From an economic perspective, public service regulation seeks to secure four basic objectives: sustainability, allocative efficiency, productive efficiency, and equity.[3]

Economic and financial sustainability implies that tariffs should generate enough revenue to allow an efficient firm to cover the economic costs of service provision. When referring to economic costs (as opposed to accounting costs), a just and fair rate of return on the capital invested in the provision of the service is explicitly included.

Allocative efficiency requires that—in an environment of scarce resources and alternative uses for them—tariffs equal service production costs. Strictly speaking, allocative efficiency requires that tariffs reflect their marginal costs. Under natural monopoly conditions, however, a firm would not cover its average production costs, so there is a need to reconcile these objectives.

Productive efficiency relates to the minimization of costs at a certain production level or the maximization of output given the amount of inputs. A firm's incentives to minimize costs will depend on the rules used to adjust tariffs in the future. There is a trade-off here between allocative efficiency and productive efficiency, because incentives can only be created by breaking a link—if only temporarily—between a firm's costs and tariffs.

Equity or distributive efficiency relate to access and affordability. Many regulatory regimes have universal service access as a medium- or long-term goal. For many essential infrastructure services, the need to relate tariffs to the poorest users' capacity to pay is well accepted.

Simplicity, certainty, consistency, and price stability are also important elements of many regulatory regimes. Given that, to a large extent, regulation involves dealing with conflicting interests of the parties involved (actual, potential, and future users; firms; government; lenders), the formal and procedural aspects of any regulatory decision are as important as the substantive aspects. For example, the formal principles considered relevant to the derivation of regulatory decisions of the Independent Pricing and Regulatory Tribunal (IPART) of New South Wales, Australia, are the following:

- *Simplicity.* Deriving the optimal approach for regulatory decisions may be a complex task. All things remaining constant, a simple approach that approximates a more complex calculation should be preferred.
- *Certainty and consistency.* The efficiency of investment in regulated activities is enhanced by consistency in decisions across time and, absent strong grounds to do otherwise, adherence to previous commitments. The ease with which an approach can be replicated from one regulatory period to the next may be an important contributor to certainty and consistency.
- *Price stability.* All else remaining constant, a lower variance in prices over time and more equal intertemporal allocation of common costs across customers may be preferred.[4]

Achieving these objectives and the trade-offs they require makes regulation an information-intensive activity. Moreover, regulation features a strong information asymmetry between the firm and the regulator in relation to the regulated firm's underlying costs, market prospects, and (to the regulator) unobservable actions.

1.2. External and internal regulatory information

One classification of the information needed for regulation is based on the source from which the information is obtained. This classification differentiates between information originating in the firm and information from other sources.[5]

Information originating in the firm

The main source of information on unregulated activities is the accounting information generated by the firm. The firm generates financial accounting aimed at external parties (information to be used by shareholders, the financial community, fiscal administrations, the public) and management accounting or cost accounting aimed at internal parties (management; see chapter 3).

Accounting in general is defined as a system for classifying the economic events occurring in a business. It deals with recording, classifying, and summarizing the economic operations of a business to establish a firm's financial capacity; and with interpreting the results. Therefore, accounting provides a means for investors, managers, and directors to follow the course of their businesses (see box 1.1). Ideally, it provides an accurate picture of a firm's stability and creditworthiness, the flow of collections and payments, the trends in sales, overall costs and expenses, and so on. Importantly, accounting information constitutes an integrated body of consistent information.

Accounting information is governed by general rules aimed at determining the basic elements that must be included to meet its objectives.

Economic theory states that the use of the firm's own economic and financial data create incentive problems.[6] Some regulatory regimes therefore seek to minimize the use of the firm's own information. Such is the case, for example, of efficient-firm regulation (which originated in the electricity sector in Chile and then spread to Peru, Bolivia, and other countries in Latin America).[7] A similar approach was adopted in the U.S. telecommunications sector through the use of cost models such as the model developed by the Federal Communications Commission to determine interconnection charges. Although this approach might appear to solve the incentives problem, it does not properly take into account economic sustainability objectives. Its use may be most relevant to the telecommunications sector in which competition in the market is the norm and sustainability concerns are not central for the regulator.

Box 1.1. General objectives of external financial reporting by business companies

Financial reporting should provide information that helps current and potential investors, creditors, and other users do the following:

- Make rational investment, credit, and similar decisions. The information should be comprehensible to those who have a reasonable understanding of business and economic activities and who are willing to study the information with reasonable diligence.
- Assess the amounts, timing, and uncertainty of prospective cash receipts from dividends or interest and the proceeds from the sale, redemption, or maturity of securities or loans. Because investors' and creditors' cash flows are related to enterprise cash flows, financial reporting should provide information to help investors, creditors, and others assess the amounts, timing, and uncertainty of prospective net cash inflows to the related enterprise.
- Assess the economic resources of an enterprise; the claims to those resources (obligations of the enterprise to transfer resources to other entities and owners' equity); and the effects of transactions, events, and circumstances that change the enterprise's resources and claims to those resources.

Source: U.S. Financial Standards Accounting Board, Concepts Statement No. 1, *Objectives of Financial Reporting by Business Enterprises* (first issued in 1978).

However, as long as economic and financial sustainability is an objective, regulation has to use the firm's own data on costs, revenues, assets, and liabilities.[8] The main source of information, though clearly not the only one, is the firm's accounting information. The requirement to use this information is reinforced by the position adopted by the courts in a range of countries that have regarded the actual costs and financial condition of the utility as key elements to be taken into account by the regulator.

The nature of "traditional" financial accounting information and some basic underlying principles of accounting in general make these data useful from a regulatory standpoint but far from sufficient. This chapter discusses some of the elements differentiating the regulator's needs from needs met by traditional accounting information.

Information originating outside the firm

Public service regulation cannot be based exclusively on information from the firm itself. To meet different regulatory objectives, the regulator must have information on the demand for and supply of the regulated service from outside the firm as well.

With respect to supply, the regulator needs to be able to determine whether the firm's costs are consistent with an appropriate level of efficiency. Therefore, the regulator needs information on available technologies and reasonable service costs to assess the firm's relative efficiency. The regulator can rely on either technological information or efficiency benchmark studies.

The regulator needs to thoroughly understand the functioning of the regulated sector, its technologies, and their application. The object is not to micromanage the firm, but to assess the firm's proposals from a technical and an economic perspective. Information on standard costs of products and typical processes are examples of important elements to be considered in the determination of efficient cost levels.

In recent years regulators have emphasized the use of efficiency frontiers (applying data envelope analysis or total factor productivity methods) as a useful tool for reducing information asymmetry.[9] Clearly, these studies are possible only when there is homogeneous information about a relatively large number of firms in the same sector or activity (to determine the relative efficiency of each firm) and over a relatively long period of time (to get measures of technological change over time). This need calls for unification of the criteria used to collect both accounting and extra-accounting information, to ensure its homogeneity and comparability and to achieve a high degree of consistency of information over time.

The regulator also requires detailed information about the demand for goods and services faced by the regulated firm. Achieving allocative efficiency and equity, in particular, calls for detailed information about users' behavior.

Regulators need reliable information about expected demand in the medium term. Revenue may vary directly with demand but, because of the fixed nature of many infrastructure costs, current costs may not vary greatly with variations in demand. Thus changes in demand can have a significant impact on the economic performance of infrastructure companies.

The greatest impact of demand variations on company expenses is on the amount and timing of investments. The indivisibility and long construction times of many infrastructure facilities make it necessary to decide on their construction long (typically several years) before they are to commence operations. Therefore, an optimal expansion plan requires the ability to estimate demand quite accurately for a good number of years into the future.

Quantities demanded by users depend directly on price through a parameter known as *price elasticity*.[10] Consequently, the quantities consumed are to some extent endogenous to the tariffs set by the regulator. This finding has an important impact on the sustainability of the service.

Equity objectives seek to ensure access and affordable tariffs for infrastructure services for the poorest segments of society. Although public service tariffs are not the best instrument of social policy, and output-based aid is a more efficient and transparent means of achieving equity objectives, in many cases fiscal and budgetary constraints limit the alternatives of direct subsidies and tariffs. Access prices that explicitly account for the conditions of poor users may be appropriate.

Whether cross-subsidies, promotion funds, or some other forms of access subsidy are used, efficient implementation requires detailed information about the consumption patterns of the users to whom these policies are targeted. Capacity and willingness-to-pay studies represent essential elements of an efficient tariff policy seeking to meet the access and service needs of poor users.

That this information is often necessary for regulatory purposes does not mean that it must be generated directly by the regulator. Indeed, much of this information, or the data needed to estimate it, is routinely produced by statistical agencies or other government organizations or research centers. Regulators can use their limited resources efficiently by identifying information sources and adjusting available data to meet their own needs.

1.3. Limitations of traditional accounting information for regulatory purposes

Traditional accounting information and some of the basic underlying principles of accounting make this information useful for regulatory purposes. Nevertheless, regulatory purposes differentiate the regulator's needs from needs met by traditional accounting information in several areas:

- Financial accounting information focuses on the firm, whereas the regulator focuses mainly on the regulated activities of the firm. From a regulatory perspective, the coexistence of regulated and unregulated activities within the firm calls for the separation of the costs and revenue of the two types of activities. Moreover, some firms may engage in activities subject to regulation by different regulators. Separation of information related to each of the activities, but particularly to the regulated and unregulated activities, places an important limitation on traditional accounting when used by the regulator.
- The focus of accounting within a firm may not be sufficient when a regulator regulates more than one firm in the same activity. Applying certain regulatory tools, such as yardstick competition, calls for a degree of homogeneity in the identification of accounts that is not always achieved by generally accepted accounting principles. See box 1.2 for a typical example of this problem.
- Accounting is usually based on a temporal cost imputation rule that may not always reflect regulatory needs. The regulator can determine tariffs that allow the recovery of costs when these costs are incurred or when the costs would be recognized in the financial accounts of the firm. Most regulatory agencies do not allow an asset to be included in the asset base until the asset is in service. To cover the financial costs associated with long-maturity projects, regulatory practice allows capitalization of the financial costs incurred during construction (AFUDC—allowance for funds used during construction). This strategy also departs from the accounting practices of unregulated firms and from generally accepted accounting principles.
- General accounting principles are inadequate for dealing with common costs that need to be allocated not only among different regulated services, but also between the regulated and unregulated activities of the firm because different allocation criteria will substantially affect the achievement of regulatory objectives.[11] A regulated firm would have strong incentives to allocate common costs to its regulated activity rather than to any of its competitive activities.

These examples are only illustrative examples of the limitations of traditional accounting data for regulatory purposes. These limitations make it necessary to complement generally accepted accounting principles with specific rules and norms that make accounting information useful for regulation purposes.

Box 1.2. Cost structures of gas companies in Argentina: The importance of homogeneity across firms in the identification of accounts

Gas Natural Ban (Gasban) and Metrogas are two of nine natural gas distribution companies in Argentina. Both provide services in Buenos Aires and are similar in number of customers and market share. The table below shows their cost structures as they appear in their balance sheets.

	1996		1998		2000	
GASBAN	**Amount share (M$)**	**Amount share (%)**	**Amount share (M$)**	**Amount share (%)**	**Amount share (M$)**	**Amount share (%)**
Administrative expenses	15,406	31.0	9,311	20.4	9,893	18.6
Sales expenses	34,317	69.0	36,253	79.6	43,260	81.4
Total	49,723		45,564		53,153	
METROGAS						
Administrative expenses	52,649	76.8	48,572	74.1	31,271	44.8
Sales expenses	15,905	23.2	16,940	25.9	38,539	55.2
Total	68,554		65,512		69,810	

The difference in the accounting cost structure of the two companies is great: proportions of administrative expenses and sales expenses are nearly reversed. Some of this difference may be due to differences in the markets served by the two companies. Another cause might be different classification criteria—although both sets of criteria are consistent with generally accepted accounting principles. From a regulatory standpoint, comparison of the accounting cost structure of the companies is extremely difficult. The regulator loses the use of a fundamental tool such as yardstick competition.

Source: Author.

In some cases, a system of management or cost accounting more elaborate than that the firm is using may be needed to properly identify the revenues and costs associated with regulated activities and unregulated activities. In other cases, management may already collect similar information for its own purposes, and regulatory compliance may entail reallocations or modifications of existing cost allocation rules for the purpose of harmonization with regulatory requirements.

Specific cost-recording and allocation rules will clearly depend on the regulated sector, its sectoral and institutional organization (number of companies within the regulator's scope, extent of competition among the different segments, extent of vertical integration, and the like), and particular features of the regulatory regime (price caps, cost of service, hybrid systems). Development of these specific rules—in a manner as consistent as possible with generally accepted accounting principles—is the aim of regulatory accounting.

The need for information for regulation goes beyond accounting data. Regulation also requires information related to physical aspects of the service (employees, productive units) and various dimensions of the quality of the service (number and duration of outages, water pressure, variations in voltage, rugosity of roads, punctuality of services).

This information is not costless. The regulator must define precisely the acceptable bases for cost allocations and the formats and content of information presented, as well as detailed processes for sharing and validating that information. Validation is itself a demanding process. Most private operators think that because their accounting data have been validated by their auditors and their board, the regulator is not entitled to reassess the data. This belief is a major point of possible misunderstanding of the regulator's role. Accounting data that are valid from a legal and fiscal point of view are not necessarily valid from an economic point of view. One of the duties of a regulator is to validate the operator's data economically (proper allocation of revenues and costs, efficient level of costs). But the requirement should be cost effective and no more stringent than necessary.

In summary, regulatory accounting should be considered an important element within a system of regulatory information. This system would include the firm's own information—both accounting and extra-accounting—and external information that is also necessary for regulation. Moreover, the design of the requirements should have regard for existing accounting systems and the cost of compliance.

1.4. Information exchange and participation: The need for processes and mechanisms

In addition to the quantitative information described above, the regulator requires information about the preferences and opinions of the regulatory system's players (users, firms, investors, government, unions).

Because regulation must deal with competing objectives and multiple trade-offs, the process used to collect the information and to make decisions is as important as the technical know-how for tariff setting. In this respect, the various mechanisms for public consultation and dispute resolution play a leading role.

Consultation documents and public hearings are two instruments that regulators can use to learn about the opinions and preferences of stakeholders in the regulatory process. These instruments contribute not only to information collection, but also to public perceptions of the regulator's performance. An open, transparent, and participatory process is essential for public legitimization of regulation.

The long-term nature of the regulatory relationship between the firm and the regulator implies that information problems will recur. From the outset of the regulatory process—ideally before private participation takes place—considerable effort should go into determining the rules that will govern the management and interchange of information. To maintain value, that initial investment in information gathering must be regularly updated, improved, and optimized throughout the life of the regulatory contract.

Notes

1. See Berg and Tschirhart (1988) for a theoretical explanation and an account of the history of regulation in the United States.

2. Eliminating information from the regulatory process was not at all the view of some of the key players in the UK regulatory system. Beesley and Littlechild (1989) argue that to conduct the "twin tasks of controlling prices and promoting competition, the regulator thus needs to acquire adequate information concerning the scope for cost reductions and the extent and effects of new entry" (p. 29). "The generation and dissemination of information are therefore at the heart of regulatory effectiveness" (p. 58).

3. Estache and others (2002) contains a detailed discussion of regulatory objectives and instruments.

4. See www.ipart.nsw.gov.au.

5. For further discussion on this topic, see Estache and Burns (1999a and 1999b).

6. See Laffont and Tirole (1994) for a model with a detailed theoretical discussion of incentives problems in regulation.

7. Efficient-firm regulation focuses on incentives to achieve productive efficiency and allocative efficiency (dynamic or long term). Financial sustainability is not properly accounted for in this approach, although in the electricity sector in Chile there is an overall test of the revenue generated to the firms in the sector by tariffs determined on the basis of the efficient firm. However, this test has such a large margin (internal rate of return between 4 percent and 12 percent) that it does not properly meet the sustainability objective. See Galetovic and Bustos (2004) for a theoretical discussion of efficient-firm regulation in the Chilean context.

8. See Grifell-Tatjé and Lovell (2003) for the standard practice of benchmarking actual managerial performance against best practice standards established by engineers. They find the consultancy's ideal distribution network to be much less costly to operate. When they decompose the cost differential into three sources, they find that the superior network design combined with lower input prices accounts for more than all of the predicted cost savings. They also find that incumbent managers are more cost efficient than the consultancy, and they speculate that the superior cost efficiency of the incumbent managers is due in part to the engineering difficulty of creating an "ideal" distribution network.

9. See Coelli and others (2003) for an introduction to efficiency measurement in public utilities, and Rossi and Ruzzier (2001) for an analysis of the use of efficiency measures in regulation.

10. Formally, price elasticity is the percentage variation in the quantity demanded after a 1 percent change in the price of the good.

11. The mere existence of both regulated activities and unregulated activities within a firm assumes some degree of complementarity or economies of scope between them; otherwise, the firm would not need to develop the activities jointly. This leads to the existence of common costs.

Chapter 2

Case Studies

This chapter illustrates some of the main issues relating to regulatory information and regulatory accounting through three case studies. The first case describes the recent privatization of an African country's only water and electricity operator through the sale of a majority stake and the granting of a 20-year concession. One year after the privatization, a controversy over the indexation formula revealed many problems, including misunderstandings of and weaknesses in the contract. The second case focuses on a Latin American country's electricity distribution sector and on information related to the separation of activities into regulated and unregulated activities. The third case presents the information problem in the water and sanitation sector in another Latin American country, where regulation is enforced on the basis of a theoretically efficient model ("ideal operator").

2.1. Case study 1: Privatization of an electricity and water operator in Africa—Initial contract not sufficiently specific

This case, involving a generally well-designed legal regulatory framework for a concession contract, illustrates two common problems: the lack of visibility of tariffs, and parties' poor understanding of regulatory requirements and information needs.

An African country decided to privatize its water and electricity operator. Following a bidding process, the state sold the majority of its shares to a foreign operator and granted the company a 20-year concession in two separate contracts, one for water services and one for electricity services.

Before the contracts were signed, a legal framework was established. The contrast between the general philosophy for the development of the sector and the main regulatory rules was clear. In addition, a law created an independent regulatory authority and stated its general rights and duties.

Tariffs were determined at the start of the concession and were to be indexed each year using a contractual indexation formula.

Information requirements

The laws and the concession contract state general obligations for the delivery of information. They also require implementation of a cost accounting system that separates water and electricity activities and subactivities (production, transport, and distribution). The law creating the regulatory authority states its powers in terms of information collection.

Powers of the regulatory authority

An article on the powers of the regulatory authority mentions that

> To fulfill its missions of control and monitoring of the agreements and tariffs [missions stated in the same law], the authority has the largest powers of investigation in the framework of the laws in force. The authority can request—from any public administration, user or operator—all the necessary information to ensure the fulfillment of the obligations imposed to them, without any limitation being imposed to it.

Obligations stated in the contract and in the law

Among the obligations stated in the contract and in the law are those covering standard accounting and cost accounting, operating and financial reports, and assets.

Standard accounting and cost accounting. The law on organization of the electricity sector states explicitly that

> every operator carrying on vertically or horizontally integrated activities will hold in its internal accounting separate accounts for each activity of production, transport and distribution and, if appropriate, for all activities not related to the electricity sector, in the same way as if these activities were carried on by separate legal entities.

No similar accounting obligations are specified for the water sector.

The concession contract contains one general article related to standard accounting and cost accounting. It states that the operator should implement a general accounting system in conformity with legal obligations, while also following the accounting principles specifically applicable to the concession regime.

Regarding cost accounting and auditing, the article states as follows:

In regards to the law, the Operator has to put in place—within a period of two years—a cost accounting system ["comptabilité analytique" in French] enabling the monitoring of the conceded service operations with a strict separation between the activities of production, transport, and distribution of electricity as well as of other activities. [This obligation of separate accounts is formally stated in the law as well.] This separation is to be realized following the accounting rules imposed by the regulatory authority after consultation with the concessionaire. These accounting rules determine the conditions following which the costs and charges of each of the activities (production, transport and distribution) are reflected in the corresponding accounting statements, in order to prevent any cross-subsidy between these activities.

Implementation of a cost accounting system is essential to regulation. This implementation is explained in chapter 5, after the basics of cost accounting are explained in chapter 4. The need for accounting rules defined by the regulatory authority after consultation with the concessionaire is covered in chapters 5 and 6.

Operating and financial reports. Another article of the contract describes the contents of an operating and financial report to be delivered to the regulatory authority and to the government. It mentions a detailed list of indicators to be included. The article adds to the list "any indicator commonly defined that helps to assess the technical and financial performances of the Company."

Assets. One article tackles the accounting treatment of categories of assets depending on the classification of assets, as shown in table 2.1.[1]

This definition of assets is related to the valuation of the regulatory asset base and the regulatory depreciation policies, covered in chapter 6.

Conflict and solutions

A conflict arose a few years after the concession started.[2] The world price of fuel rose drastically, but the parties did not agree on the tariff increases to be applied on

Table 2.1. Classification of assets in concession contract

	Conceded assets		Private assets	
Essential assets	Renewable	Nonrenewable	Renewable	Nonrenewable
Nonessential assets	Renewable	Nonrenewable	Renewable	Nonrenewable

Source: Authors.
Note: Conceded assets belong to the state but are conceded to the operator. *Private assets* belong to the operator. *Essential assets* are essential to the activity and must be returned or sold to the state at the end of the concession. *Nonessential assets* are not essential to the activity and might be handed over to or sold to the state at the end of the concession. *Renewable assets* are to be renewed during the concession (the asset's life ends before the concession ends). *Nonrenewable assets* cannot be renewed during the concession (the asset's life ends after the concession ends).

the basis of the indexation formula. Problems with other ratios and weights used in the formula also arose. The conflict revealed multiple misunderstandings. Table 2.2 categorizes the main issues highlighted in this case study and notes if and where they are discussed in this volume.

The parties finally decided that one way to resolve the conflict and the misunderstandings about the profitability of the operator was to construct an economic-financial model. All the parties (regulator, operator, and ministry of energy and water) were to be involved in developing the model. (For more details on developing such a model, see annex 2 on regulatory modeling.)

Approval by all parties of the structure and mechanisms of the model was relatively conflict free, but tensions arose during data collection from the operator, which believed that the requirements were too detailed. The process revealed the incompleteness of the cost accounting system. The most difficult stage was final validation of the data by the regulator and the government. This process requires considerable work, analysis, and judgment. The operator appeared unable to understand that some costs that the regulator considered inefficient might be excluded in the determination of future tariffs. This topic is considered in chapter 5.

2.2. Case study 2: Regulating operators in Latin America—Manual deficiencies led to inconsistent cost accounting by different utilities

The electricity sector in this Latin American country is composed of several independent electricity distribution companies regulated by a single agency. This case focuses on information related to the separation in the distribution business of

Table 2.2. Issues highlighted in case study 1 and where they are discussed in this volume

Issue	Problem	Where topic is discussed
Technical issues	• Flaws and contradictions in contract • Poor design of indexation formula and weak understanding of regulatory mechanisms and efficiency by both parties • Delivered information incomplete (cost accounting system in place on time) and partially inappropriate or inconsistent	• Legal drafting errors are not covered in this volume • Specific technical issue of the design of indexation formulas is not covered in this volume. • Standard basic information needs are covered in chapter 5 on regulatory accounting; information exchange processes are covered in chapter 7.
Conceptual issues	• No mutual comprehension of economic and financial justification of the tariffs	• Annex 2 on modeling explains how an economic-financial model is essential for justifying the average tariffs and designing a fair tariff policy for different categories of users.
Processes	• Poor comprehension of the roles of the government and the regulatory authority in the relationship with the operator • Poor comprehension of regulatory concepts by the operator and the government • No formal information exchange process and no accurate definition of information needs	• The legal status of the regulatory authority and its institutional role are tackled in chapter 7. • Basic regulatory concepts are tackled in the introduction (other references provided). • Need to share knowledge and information with operator, along with need for regulatory accounting guidelines and exchange rules and mechanisms, is covered in chapter 7.

Source: Authors.

regulated activities and unregulated activities. It illustrates how, in a large and complex sector, fundamental information is missing on unregulated activities.

The chart of accounts (see chapter 3) included in the "Accounting Manual for Electricity Public Services" foresees the need for an accounting separation of regulated activities from unregulated activities:

Concessionaires and licensees performing activities not related to the concession of Electricity Public Services must keep separate registers and controls of all operations related to such activities. Moreover, joint undertakings [business associations] for any purpose or condition as well as investments in other companies should also be considered within this concept.

It is considered that activities not related to a concession of Electricity Public Services are said to be all the operations carried out by the Concessionaire and licensee not directly related to the object of the Concession, that is, business activities different from electricity Generation, Transmission, Distribution and Trading.

It is the Concessionaire or licensee's job to define the criteria for identification and separation of goods, rights and obligations, as well as refinement of the respective revenue resulting from these activities not related to the concession of Electricity Public Services. These criteria, however, need to be subjected to the approval of the Regulatory Entity before being applied. Moreover, it is important that these criteria consider the issue of allowing disclosure of the information available in the guidelines for preparation and publication of accounting, economic and financial and social reports.

The rules mentioned before shall operate without detriment to the specific provisions contained in the respective regulations which establish the need of procuring the Regulator's approval for the performance of activities not related to the object of the concession or licensee.

Table 2.3 identifies the relevant variables from the Accounting Manual.

Only 21 electricity distribution companies had data for the separate accounts. These companies represent 58 percent of users and 54 percent of electricity consumption. Table 2.4 shows details for the companies for which at least some information is available.

Most of these accounts show incomplete data. Although many of the 21 companies provide information on expenses for activities unrelated to the concession,

Table 2.3. Accounting information required for unregulated activities

BEFORE TAXES (SOCIAL CONTRIBUTION AND INCOME TAX)

Operating

1. Operating income from activities not related to the concession
2. Operating expenses from activities not related to the corcession

Nonoperating

3. Nonoperating income from activities not related to the concession
4. Nonoperating expenses from activities not related to the concession

AFTER TAXES (SOCIAL CONTRIBUTIONS AND INCOME TAX)

5. Profits and losses of the year, from activities not related to the concession

Source: Authors.

only nine of the companies register revenue from unregulated operating or nonoperating activities. That companies would have costs associated with unregulated activities but no revenue related to them appears improbable.

Table 2.5 categorizes the main issues highlighted in this case study and notes where they are discussed in this volume.

2.3. Case study 3: Efficient model company regulation in a Latin American country — Deficiencies of benchmarking information and the need for regulatory accounting information

Regulation of the water and sanitation sector in this Latin American country is governed by a regulatory framework set out in a law that created an independent regulatory authority as part of the restructuring of the country's sanitation services in the late 1980s. The regulator is a decentralized public agency with ruling, controlling, and sanctioning powers. It is responsible for supervision of service providers, enforcement of sanitation rules and regulations, control of liquid industrial wastes, and tariff setting for regulated services.

Table 2.4. Accounting information on unregulated activities, 2001

Company	Control	Users 2001	Energy 2001	Operating income of activities not related to concession (thousands)	Expenses of activities not related to concession (thousands)	Non-operating income of activities not related to concession (thousands)	Non-operating expenses of activities not related to concession (thousands)	Operating income (thousands)	Operating expenses (thousands)	Non-operating income (thousands)	Non-operating expenses (thousands)
EMP-1	STATE	1,228,554	3,470,470	237.0	(665.9)	215.8	(211.1)	536,084	(542,883)	5,721.3	(9,924.6)
EMP-2	STATE	5,412,068	11,715,540	7,319.8	(5,192.5)	0.2	(566.0)	1,910,598	(1,468,129)	498.0	(12,559.4)
EMP-3	STATE	116,306	288,086	3.5	(0.2)	—	—	42,343	(42,213)	9.1	(632.8)
EMP-4	STATE	145,155	242,241	—	(21.6)	—	—	65,602	(92,901)	106.4	(78.2)
EMP-5	PRIVATE	5,437	15,529	—	—	—	(1.9)	1,238	(920)	1.3	(2.5)
EMP-6	PRIVATE	37,878	97,090	—	—	2.2	(2.2)	10,977	(8,399)	2.9	(179)
EMP-7	PRIVATE	90,324	254,453	—	—	2.2	(627.7)	26,388	(31,830)	5.1	(673.1)
EMP-8	PRIVATE	132,174	361,985	—	—	—	(433.1)	31,158	(37,818)	70.1	(815.9)
EMP-9	PRIVATE	145,935	403,680	—	—	—	(2.3)	43,713	(37,087)	48.0	(370.9)
EMP-10	PRIVATE	172,411	467,748	—	—	14.4	(1,081.2)	48,114	(51,161)	23.7	(2,129.9)
EMP-11	PRIVATE	281,059	586,284	—	—	—	(29.4)	70,146	(56,125)	423.2	(184.1)
EMP-12	PRIVATE	403,232	632,400	—	(6,113.4)	—	—	90,031	(74,776)	77.9	(105.4)
EMP-13	PRIVATE	572,320	1,620,244	—	(29.4)	—	—	171,946	(152,810)	231.9	(1,914.8)
EMP-14	PRIVATE	728,855	1,295,538	—	(3,926.4)	—	386.4	174,782	(146,017)	102.0	62.2
EMP-15	PRIVATE	1,044,379	2,288,533	—	(30.9)	—	—	257,936	(229,621)	2,649.0	(339.9)
EMP-16	PRIVATE	1,691,224	3,990,374	—	(0.3)	—	—	637423	(477,379)	4378	(268.4)
EMP-17	PRIVATE	1,716,558	4,426,719	546.0	(17,463.2)	—	—	631,567	(557,924)	852.1	(3,700.8)
EMP-18	PRIVATE	1,916,760	2,898,281	—	(15,774.6)	—	—	364,038	(278,289)	879.5	(1,350.6)
EMP-19	PRIVATE	2,918,419	4,858,335	—	(4,926.2)	—	—	575,169	(500,747)	1,574.7	(536.1)
EMP-20	PRIVATE	3,233,040	10,135,359	—	—	7,024.3	—	1,881,153	(1,534,926)	7,049.7	(4,835.0)
EMP-21	PRIVATE	4,748,947	16,862,369	—	(2,002.7)	8,352.9	(8,341.4)	2,334,596	(2,078,059)	10,033.2	(16,887.2)
Share		58%	54%								

Source: Compiled by authors.

Table 2.5. Issues discussed in case study 2 and where they are discussed in this volume

Issue	Problem	Where topic is discussed
Discretion	• The criteria to identify and classify unregulated activities should be defined by the regulator and not by the operators, as stated in the accounting manual.	• Separation of activities is discussed in chapter 6.
Quality of information	• Information received from the operators is not used by the regulator. • There is no audit of information.	• The role of regulator is discussed in chapter 5. • Information exchange processes are discussed in chapter 7.
Comparability	• Need for homogeneous criteria allowing for yardstick competition.	• Regulatory accounting guidelines are covered in chapter 7.
Materiality	• Values reported are not significant.	• Materiality is tackled in chapter 3 and again in chapter 7.

Source: Authors.

The regulatory framework

The regulatory framework relies on two basic economic principles: economic and dynamic efficiency and financial feasibility, which requires that sanitation utilities be self-financing. To encourage economic efficiency, tariffs are determined in accordance with the efficient model company approach. Tariffs are set on the basis of independent costs, which may differ from the actual costs of utilities.

Under the sector regulatory framework, tariffs must reflect the cost of capturing, carrying, treating, and distributing drinkable water and the costs arising from the collection, treatment, and disposal of wastewater. As for other public services in the country, social goals are met by a nationwide scheme of direct subsidies.

During each tariff review, the efficient model company approach imagines that a company is starting from scratch. Only the essential costs of service provision are taken into account. Investment costs are separated from operation and maintenance costs. Investments are calculated on the basis of an engineering model that ensures technical feasibility and assumes the most efficient technology available in the market. Operation and maintenance costs are estimated on the basis of the actual companies and in consideration of industry best practices. The need to have information about real companies arises in the context of cost estimation. In the last few years, companies have become more diversified, and the absence of key elements in the framework for the design of dynamic mechanisms of information disclosure has become more evident.

Regulators found themselves even more limited by the firms' traditional financial accounting. Because companies conduct their accounting according to their management needs, accounting systems can vary year to year. Moreover, the regulated companies are heterogeneous and, therefore, so are their accounting systems. The costs of regulated activities are not separated from the costs of unregulated activities. As a result, financial accounting does not provide the necessary indicators to support a tariff study.

A new regulatory accounting model

To get around these limitations, the regulator issued a form for submitting information related to water costs and revenues and a formal protocol for exchanging information. The regulatory accounting model set out by these regulations follows an activity-based costing allocation method, adjusted to meet regulatory needs. The cost of each product or service is determined on the basis of the activities needed for its development and the resources used by each activity. The analysis is carried out at standard facility (operation and maintenance), location (commercial), and company (administrative) levels.

These information requirements are limited to the firms' operation and maintenance costs and do not include asset accounts. The firms' investments are not considered for tariff setting. An engineering model of an efficient company is used for that purpose.

The regulated companies had several complaints about these information requirements. Some complaints were based on technical aspects, such as inconsistency between the instructions given by the regulator and the firm's chart of accounts. Regulated companies also raised economic objections. They argued that the spirit of the regulatory framework was changed and that the efficient model company approach did not include the cost of generating information in the determination of tariffs. Furthermore, some companies argued that the regulator lacked the authority to impose a specific regulatory accounting system or to ask for information about unregulated products. These objections and some lawsuits filed in court were eventually rejected, and the plan proposed by the regulator became effective in 2004.

Two points about this case are especially relevant here. One is the impossibility of developing efficient regulation without taking into account the information generated by the company and the need to rule on the information that can be used for regulatory purposes. The other is the particularity of this case: the information required was limited to operation and maintenance costs and excluded the firms' accounts of capital. This limitation on the information could lead to an inconsistency across all cost elements considered for tariff setting. This differentiated regulatory treatment between investments on the one hand and operation and maintenance costs on the other hand could result in strategic behavior by firms—that is, give them an incentive to consider investments as costs.

Table 2.6 categorizes the main issues highlighted in this case study and notes where they are discussed in this volume.

Table 2.6. Issues discussed in case study 3 and where they are discussed in this volume

Issue	Problem	Where topic is discussed
Powers of the regulator to acquire information	• Regulators need specific powers to fulfill their duties, including the power to collect information from service providers	• Regulatory accounting guidelines are covered in chapter 7.
Relationship between regulatory regime and information needed by the regulator	• Data requirements by the regulator depend on the characteristics of each regulatory regime	• Covered in chapter 2.
Need for an integrated approach for treating economic and financial data	• Limiting the regulatory accounting requirements to operation and maintenance costs and excluding capital expenditure limits the usefulness of the information	• Regulatory asset base and depreciation are covered in chapter 6.
Use of activity-based costing as a basis for the regulatory accounting model	• Values reported are not significant	• Allocation methods accounting approaches, including activity-based costing, are covered in chapter 4.

Source: Authors.

Notes

1. This classification of assets is stated in the law as well. This kind of classification is common in the countries belonging to the Economic Community of West African States.

2. For more details on conflicts arising early in concession contracts, see Guasch (2004).

Chapter 3

Corporate Information and Financial Accounting

This chapter is for individuals unfamiliar with basic accounting principles and concepts. Those who already understand these topics can skip it without loss of continuity. The chapter briefly describes the main elements of a corporate information system and the basic principles of financial accounting. References at the end of the chapter direct readers to more detailed discussions of these topics.

3.1. Corporate information systems

Information is an essential business tool. Companies require information to control their activities, make decisions, create new services and products, and evaluate expansion possibilities. Information is developed through models and methods that allow movement from a set of unconnected data to adequate and timely information at each administrative level.

To make information consistent with the objectives for which it is required, information systems are used to organize information according to a set of attributes related to time, content, and form. An information system can be defined as "a group of interrelated components working together to *collect, process, store, and disseminate* information to support decision making and control it in an organization" (Loudon and Loudon 1998, 8).

An efficient and properly managed company operating at a substantial level should implement corporate information systems for management (planning, evaluation, control) and nonmanagement groups (tax authorities, various regulatory agencies, or other governmental entities requiring customized reporting of data).

An information system receives data as input from the company's internal and external sources, processes the data to produce information, and produces information for future use by managers, administrators, shareholders, creditors, governments, and others (figure 3.1).

In general, the objectives of corporate information systems are to

- support business operations and managerial decision making,
- contribute to the automation of the company's activities and processes,
- provide information to units in the company in the form and at the time it is needed,
- provide a diagnosis of the company at a certain time, and
- aid in business forecasting.

Information systems can be formal (based on standardized procedures) or informal (based on unstated or loosely stated rules and agreements). Formal systems are usually supported by electronic means and include four subsystems: production, marketing, human resources management, and financial and accounting. Each subsystem can be defined as a unit working through interfaces to exchange information with other subsystems to meet a specific goal.

This chapter focuses on financial and accounting information; chapter 4 examines management and cost accounting. The financial and accounting system is the major source of quantitative information for every company. It provides information for internal and external reporting.

Internal reporting

Internal reporting focuses on management planning and control and is usually referred to as *management accounting*. As defined by the American National Association of Accountants (quoted in Shim and Siegel [2000, 3]),

> *management accounting is the process of identification, measurement, accumulation, analysis, preparation, interpretation, and communication of financial information, which is used by management to plan, evaluate and control within an organization.*

Management accounting can use a variety of data (financial and nonmonetary). Cost accounting focuses specifically on cost information: cost recording and reporting, cost measurement, cost management, and cost analysis.

Figure 3.1. Corporate information systems

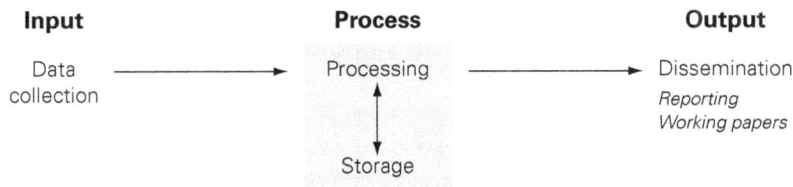

Input	Process	Output

Data collection → Processing → Dissemination

Processing ↕ Storage

Dissemination
Reporting
Working papers

Source: Authors.

External reporting

External reporting focuses principally on historical data. Such reporting is usually referred to as *financial accounting*. The main outcome of financial reporting is statutory financial statements.

3.2. Statutory financial statements

Financial statements report a company's historic financial performance and current financial position. When a company has subsidiaries, financial statements are constructed for each subsidiary, and a *consolidated financial statement* is compiled. This statement combines all the activities of the core controlling company.

Financial statements are based on financial accounting, which is concerned with classifying, measuring, and recording the transactions of a business. The financial statements of an economic entity are prepared on the basis of accounting policies, norms, and principles.

The following sections briefly present the most common generally accepted accounting principles, describe the key elements of a standard financial statement and the basic concept of the accounting plan, and survey the recent evolution of international accounting norms.

Generally accepted accounting principles

Generally accepted accounting principles (GAAP) encompass broad principles and conventions of general application, as well as rules and procedures that determine accepted accounting practices. They are used all over the world with some local variations. Each country has developed more detailed norms and accounting policies

3

Box 3.1. Some differences between the French and the Anglo-Saxon accounting approaches

One notable distinction is between the Anglo-Saxon and the French approaches to accounting.[a] General accounting influenced by the French approach privileges a contractual and patrimonial view of the company. It is also strictly regulated. The Anglo-Saxon philosophy of accounting relies principally on an economic view of the company. This type of accounting is less regulated, allowing the firm and its representatives greater freedom in organizing the details of reporting.

In some cases, these differences can influence presentation of the financial statements and valuation of accounting items such as assets. Under the French approach, assets are valued at their historical "patrimonial" value (a value recognizing the ownership of the asset but not its real economic value at the time of reporting). The Anglo-Saxon approach allows assets to be valued at an estimate of their economic value following a current cost accounting approach, as authorized in the United Kingdom (but used mainly by regulated utilities), or at historical cost.

Source: Authors.
a. The French approach is used in many European countries and in some Latin American and African countries.

(Statement of Financial Accounting Standards in the United States and Financial Reporting Standards in the United Kingdom, for example). See box 3.1 for a brief discussion of the differences between the French and Anglo-Saxon approaches.

GAAP provide guidance for preparation of financial statements along several dimensions. Some of the principles mentioned below, such as materiality and substance over form, are strongly related to basic regulatory accounting principles. The recording of transactions at historical costs has fueled many debates about the valuation of the regulatory asset base. Chapter 6 covers all these points in detail.

Basic postulate of fairness

The accounting system should present fairly and disclose fully the financial position and results of the entity's operation.

Concepts related to the socioeconomic environment

Two concepts are related to the socioeconomic environment of the entity. According to the *entity concept,* the organizational component being accounted for has to be defined—in other words, boundaries must be defined. According to the *going concern concept,* the entity is assumed to continue in operation long enough to use existing assets for their intended purpose (otherwise, termination or bankruptcy values may be lower than ongoing values).

Principles directly related to the recording of information

Four principles are related to the recording of information:

- *Conservatism.* When in doubt, accountants should choose the option least likely to result in an overstatement of income and results. For example, an accountant should value a land asset at historical cost (even if it was acquired long ago) or record it at an anticipated loss but not an anticipated gain.
- *Materiality.*[1] A transaction must be accounted for when the amounts involved are judged to be material. The materiality of the transaction must be determined by its effect on the financial statements and by whether its omission or misstatement could influence the economic decision of users.
- *Periodicity.* For the purpose of measuring profit or loss, accountants assume that the entity's life is divided into periods of time. They use fiscal periods.
- *Substance over form.* The economic substance of a transaction should be reported without regard to its form. For example, use of a capital lease to acquire an asset will not prevent the transaction from being recorded as an asset and a liability, just as would have been the case if the asset had been acquired through a long-term loan.

Principles related to valuation

Two principles are used in valuing assets and liabilities and in recording transactions. In accordance with the first principle, *historical cost and unit of measure,* assets and liabilities are recorded at historical cost in nominal currency.[2] In accordance with the second principle, *accrual accounting,* revenue is recorded in the period when sales are completed ("revenue recognition"), and expenses are recorded when resources are used to generate revenues ("the matching principle"). Thus, revenues are to be matched with related expenses. The two valuation-related principles are usually enforced by legislation or defined by professional and regulatory organizations, and they may change over time.

Key elements of statutory financial statements

Financial statements normally include three reports:

- The *balance sheet* summarizes a company's financial position at a point in time.
- The *income statement* measures a company's earnings over time, generally between balance sheets.
- The *cash flow statement* complements the income statement and balance sheet and reports the amounts of cash entering and leaving a company.

These reports are usually compiled quarterly and annually.

Balance sheet

A balance sheet summarizes a company's financial position at a point in time. Following accepted accounting practices, all companies must have a classified balance sheet. Under the fundamental accounting equation, the resources owned by a company should equal the sources of these resources, or, in accounting terms,

$$\text{Assets} = \text{liabilities} + \text{shareholders' equity.}$$

Assets are the economic resources controlled by the company. Liabilities represent the financial obligations or debt of the company or, from another point of view, the creditors' claims on the company's assets. Shareholders' equity refers to funding from shareholders provided as capital (initial capital plus later increases in capital) plus accumulated or retained earnings to shareholders (undistributed profits that are reinvested in the company).

On balance sheets, assets are classified by their *liquidity*—the time it takes to convert them into cash. *Current assets* are expected to be converted into cash or used in operations within one year or one operating cycle of the date on the balance sheet, whichever is longer. *Long-term assets* are of longer duration (more than one year or operating cycle).

Current assets. There are four common classes of current assets:

- *Cash* is the most basic current asset. In addition to currency, bank accounts without restrictions, checks, and drafts are also considered cash because of the ease with which they can be turned into currency.
- *Cash equivalents* are not cash but can be converted into cash so easily that they are considered equivalent to cash. Cash equivalents are generally highly liquid, short-term investments such as U.S. government securities and money market funds.

- *Accounts receivable* represent money that clients owe to the company.
- A company's *inventory* is the stock of products before they are sold and the stock of materials used to manufacture the products.

Long-term assets. There are two common classes of long-term assets. *Fixed assets* are tangible assets with a useful life greater than one year. Generally, fixed assets refer to items such as equipment, buildings, production plants, and property. Depreciation is the process of allocating the original purchase price of a fixed asset over the course of its useful life. It appears in the balance sheet as a deduction from the original value of the fixed assets. *Intangible assets* are nonphysical assets such as copyrights, franchises, and patents.

Liabilities. Liabilities are ordered according to their settlement. *Current liabilities* are obligations that the company must pay (from current assets) within one year of the date on the balance sheet. *Long-term liabilities* are those that are not expected to be paid for at least one year from the same date.

There are three common classes of liabilities:

- *Bank loans* are short-term debt (current liabilities) and long-term debt (noncurrent).
- *Debts to suppliers* are accounts payable to suppliers for miscellaneous supplies of goods and services (current liabilities).
- *Fiscal and social security debts* are balance of value-added taxes or sales tax due to the state for the year, income taxes, balance of company charges due on employees' remunerations, and the like (current liabilities with the exception of some deferred tax liabilities that could be listed as noncurrent).

Shareholders' equity. Shareholders' equity appears on the liabilities side of the balance sheet. It represents mainly initial funds provided by shareholders to fund the company's development and retained earnings or profits (or losses) not distributed to shareholders (when the shareholders decided to reinvest them in the company) but that belong to them. Therefore, shareholders' equity represents amounts due to the shareholders by the company or a liability. Shareholders' equity is sometimes also presented within net assets, meaning assets net of liabilities. Indeed, the amount of shareholders' equity can be calculated by subtracting the liabilities (of the different creditors) from the total assets of the company:

Shareholders' equity = assets – liabilities.

Therefore, shareholders' equity represents the net accounting value of the company, but it usually differs from the market value of the company. Assets can be recorded at historical cost (see previous section on GAAP), and the market value of some assets might be very different, positively or negatively, from the accounting value. Some assets, such as intangible assets, might not even be included in the balance sheet. In addition, the market prefers to value an operating company on the basis of its capacity to generate future profits rather than on the basis of its net accounting value. Therefore, prices paid by the market during privatization or public flotation might differ significantly from the accounting value (*net assets*).

Table 3.1 shows a simplified balance sheet. As it shows, liabilities plus shareholders' equity equal assets. The order of presentation of liabilities and shareholders' equity differ depending on accounting practices. For example, in U.S. accounting the items will usually be presented in the general order of preference in case of liquidation. Thus, in table 3.1, the liabilities of creditors are shown before shareholders' equity, because creditors would be paid before shareholders (owners) if the company were liquidated. In French accounting, the order is reversed.

Income statement

An income statement measures a company's earnings during a period of time, generally between balance sheets dates. It lists revenues, operating, financial and fiscal expenses, asset depreciation, and gains and losses. The income statement can be used to analyze profitability by applying financial ratios, or to compare profit margins with those of competitors, among others. An income statement generally contains the following components:

- *Sales* are the total amount received or to be received from the sales of products and services to customers during the period.
- *Cost of goods sold* is the total cost of products sold during the period. This cost includes the cost of raw materials, manufacturing, and labor (but not salaries). Costs of goods sold are subtracted from sales to calculate gross profit.
- *Operating expenses* are every expense other than cost of goods sold, interest, and other income tax. These expenses include research and development, marketing, salaries, and rent. Any normal expense incurred in the day-to-day operations of the company falls under this category.
- *Depreciation* is the annual amount deducted from tangible assets (such as heavy machinery used in the production of goods), representing the lifespan of the asset. It is the charge for using these assets during the period. None of this

Table 3.1. Simplified balance sheet based on the U.S. model

	2006	2005
ASSETS		
Current assets		
Cash and cash equivalents	5,000	1,000
Accounts receivable	20,000	13,000
Inventory	30,000	25,000
Total current assets	**55,000**	**39,000**
Fixed assets		
Plant and machinery	17,000	16,000
Less depreciation	−11,000	−9,000
Land	4,000	4,000
Intangible assets	3,000	1,000
Total fixed assets	13,000	12,000
TOTAL ASSETS	**68,000**	**51,000**
LIABILITIES AND SHAREHOLDERS' EQUITY		
LIABILITIES		
Accounts payable	16,000	13,000
Taxes payable	2,000	1,000
Long-term bonds issued	15,000	4,000
TOTAL LIABILITIES	**33,000**	**18,000**
SHAREHOLDERS' EQUITY		
Common stock	30,000	30,000
Retained earnings	5,000	3,000
TOTAL SHAREHOLDERS' EQUITY	**35,000**	**33,000**
LIABILITIES AND SHAREHOLDERS' EQUITY	**68,000**	**51,000**

Source: Authors.
Note: Companies in countries with different accounting practices could present items on the balance sheet in a different order.

expense amount is a cash outlay in the period recorded, which makes it a unique expense compared with other operating expenses.

- *Other income* is revenue that does not stem from the core operations of the business. This income includes items such as capital gains (or losses) from investments, foreign currency exchange, or income from the rental of property.

Table 3.2. Simplified income statement

	2006	2005
Sales	1,000,000	800,000
Cost of goods sold	−500,000	−400,000
Gross profit	**500,000**	**400,000**
Operating expenses	−100,000	−80,000
Depreciation	−20,000	−16,000
Operating income	**380,000**	**304,000**
Other income	10,000	—
Earnings before interest and tax	**390,000**	**304,000**
Interest expense	−39,000	−30,400
Net profit before taxes	**351,000**	**273,600**
Taxes (30%)	−105,300	−82,080
Net profit	**245,700**	**191,520**

Source: Authors.

- *Interest expense* is the amount of interest on debt (interest-bearing liability) for the period.
- *Income tax* is the total amount that must be paid to the government. This amount is normally calculated as a percentage (tax rate) over the taxable income of the business. Other nonincome taxes are included under operating expenses.

Table 3.2 shows a simplified income statement. The bottom line, *net profit*, shows the increase or decrease in net worth of a company before any distributions to shareholders.

Normally, sales are determined using the accrual basis of accounting. Under this method, revenues are recognized when a company sells goods or provides services, independent of cash receipt. Expenses are recognized when revenue is recorded, independent of cash payments. Although this method shows the flow of business income and debts accurately, it may not indicate the availability of cash reserves, possibly resulting in a serious cash flow problem. For instance, a company's income statement may show thousands of dollars in sales, while its bank account is empty because customers have not paid.

Cash flow statement
Complementing the balance sheet and income statement, the cash flow statement reports the amounts of cash and equivalents entering and leaving a company. The

cash flow statement allows investors to understand how a company's operations are running, where its money is coming from, and how money is being spent.

The cash flow statement is designed to convert the accrual basis of accounting used to prepare the income statement and balance sheet back to a cash basis for analyzing the actual cash flowing into and out of the business. Under accrual accounting, net income does not typically equal net cash flow, except over the lifespan of a company. Thus periodic reporting of cash inflows and outflows is important.

Cash flow is based on three components: operating activities, investing activities, and financing activities.

- *Operating activities* are the daily internal activities of a business that either require cash or generate it. Generally, changes made in cash, accounts receivable, depreciation, inventory, and accounts payable are reflected in cash from operations.
- *Investing activities* are investments made by management that consist primarily of the purchase or sale of equipment. A company's purchase of new assets is considered a cash-out transaction. When a company divests an asset, the transaction is considered cash-in for calculating cash from investing.
- *Financing activities* are external sources and uses of cash that affect cash flow. These activities include sales of common stock, changes in short- or long-term loans, and dividends paid. For example, changes in cash from financing are cash-in when capital is raised and cash-out when dividends are paid.

Table 3.3 shows a simple cash flow statement.

Chart of accounts

A chart of accounts is a listing of all accounts in the general ledger, each account accompanied by a reference number. It allows the recording of all necessary data. Box 3.2 notes two important points about charts of accounts for regulators.

The French accounting practice, with its Plan Comptable Général (PCG), takes a regulated approach to the development of a chart of accounts. Enforced legally, the PCG has a detailed fixed codification. The French approach has been adopted by many other European countries but not always as a legal obligation. Countries of the West African Economic and Monetary Union have applied versions of the PCG, such as the Système Comptable Ouest-Africain (Syscoa), since 1998.

The Anglo-Saxon accounting tradition takes a different approach to the charting of accounts. Instead of specific legal rules to be applied to a plan or codification of

Table 3.3. Simple cash flow statement

	December 2004
Net earnings	800,000
Additions to cash	
Depreciation	10,000
Decrease in accounts receivable	20,000
Increase in accounts payable	15,000
Subtractions from cash	
Decrease in taxes payable	−3,000
Increase in inventory	−30,000
Net cash from operations	812,000
Cash flow from investing	
Equipment	−30,000
Cash flow from financing	
Paid dividends	−15,000
Net cash flow	**767,000**

Source: Authors.

Box 3.2. Two important points about charts of accounts for regulators

For regulators, two points about charts of accounts are important. First, the charts provide more detailed information than general financial statements, especially on the *cost of goods and services sold* and *expense accounts.* The charts are the basic source for most accounting statements and provide detailed original information. They enable comparison of the level of specific cost items over time. In the absence of a cost accounting information system, the chart of accounts is the minimum information from which the regulator can gain some knowledge about the cost structure. However, the codification used by the company or imposed by the law might not suit the regulator's needs, and a chart of accounts *at the company level* (without segmentation of activities, for example) will not enable the regulator to verify compliance with its regulatory objectives.

Second, charts of accounts are not included in statutory financial statements. They have to be requested from the company as part of a more general information request. Chapter 6 covers this issue in more detail.

Source: Authors.

accounting transactions, more general obligations concerning the information to be provided give countries a margin of freedom. Auditors or professional organizations provide charts of account rules and principles, creating some homogeneity.

Some general principles apply to the organization of charts of accounts:

- The flow of items is from the general (starting with collective accounts) to the particular.
- Account names reflect clear terminology.
- Accounts are not overgeneralized.

Reference numbers are assigned to items logically, referring to items in terms of their recording in the appropriate financial statements: balance sheet, profit and loss account, or other statement. Usually, assets are listed first (from most to least liquid), followed by liabilities, revenues (operating income first, then nonoperating income), charges, and so on. Table 3.4 provides an example of accounts numbering in the United States.

The number of digits depends on the level of detail needed to describe the transactions. The French PCG and the West African Syscoa—where the codification is strictly defined—can use up to six digits. Table 3.5 shows the main classes used by the Syscoa chart plan.

The new International Financial Reporting Standards norms

Since 2005 all consolidated accounts of companies quoted on European stock exchanges have followed the International Financial Reporting Standards (IFRS) developed by the International Accounting Standards Board (IASB).[3]

Table 3.4. Example of accounts numbering in the United States

Class 1	1000–1999	Asset accounts
Class 2	2000–2999	Liability accounts
Class 3	3000–3999	Equity accounts
Class 4	4000–4999	Revenue accounts
Class 5	5000–5999	Cost of goods sold
Class 6	6000–6999	Expense accounts

Source: Authors.

Table 3.5. Example of the main classes of accounts numbering used in the West African Syscoa Chart Plan

Class 1	Resources (long-term liabilities)
Class 2	Fixed assets
Class 3	Stocks
Class 4	Accounts receivable
Class 5	Cash accounts
Class 6	Cost of goods and expenses ("ordinary activities")
Class 7	Revenues (from "ordinary activities")
Class 8	Other costs and revenues
(Class 9)	(Dedicated to cost accounting)

Source: Authors.

The conceptual framework of the IFRS norms closely resembles the Anglo-Saxon framework with respect to

- economic vision of the company,
- explicit integration of principles such as "substance over form" and "fair value,"
- information oriented mainly toward investors, and
- information aimed at measuring the economic performance of the company and used as a decision-making tool.

Following these norms, the concept of "fair value" is progressively applied to the valuation of all assets. Fair value is the market value of the asset at the end of each period (based on the concept of a revaluation of the asset from period to period) or, if the market value is unavailable, the exchange value or actualized value of future cash flows generated by the asset under consideration.

The West African accounting system Syscoa was influenced by the French accounting system and the PCG, but it was also influenced by the IFRS. It adopts a partial economic presentation of the assets and liabilities of the company rather than the strictly patrimonial and legal approach of the French accounting system (applying, for example, the principle of "substance over form" for some categories of assets or costs[4]). Nonetheless, Syscoa applies the historical cost concept and not the fair value concept. Applying the fair value concept involves a much higher information requirement, and information is not an easily accessible resource in Africa.

Additional reading and resources

Dufils, P., C. Lopater, and E. Guyomard. 2002. *Comptable 2003.* Mémento pratique Francis Lefebvre. Paris: Editions Francis Lefebvre.

Friedlob, G. T., and F. J. Plewa, Jr. 2000. "Financial and Business Statements." 2nd ed. Hauppauge, NY: Barron's Educational Series.

Laudon, K., and J. Laudon. 1998. *Management Information Systems: New Approaches to Organization and Technology.* 5th ed. Upper Saddle River, NJ: Prentice Hall.

Pintaux, P. 2002. "Le système comptable ouest-africain (Syscoa): L'intégration économique par la comptabilité." Tertiaire 104. Paris.

UEMOA (Union economique et monétaire ouest africaine). 1997. *Système comptable ouest africain: guide d'application.* Paris: Foucher.

Walton, P. 2001. *La comptabilité anglo-saxonne.* Paris: La Découverte.

See also International Accounting Standards Board, www.iasb.org, on IFRS norms.

Notes

1. In some countries, such as France, accounting regulation does not explicitly define materiality.

2. In the United Kingdom, companies may record fixed assets at a value higher than historical cost to compensate for the impact of inflation on long-term assets. This strategy is called *modified historical cost.* Revalued assets are then depreciated on the basis of their new value. This practice is in line with the British approach to regulatory asset base valuation (see chapter 6). However, this *current cost accounting* is not an obligation. Companies may continue to show their statements in historical cost. In practice, the main users of current cost accounting are regulated utility companies.

3. These norms are not accepted in the United States, where European companies still have to apply U.S. GAAP rules in meeting their reporting requirements.

4. The principle of "substance over form" is not formally included in the basic principles of Syscoa, because it was perceived as too far from the cultural and legal tradition of these African countries, but the principle is applied to some specific types of assets and charges. For more information, see Pintaux (2002).

3

Chapter 4

Management and Cost Accounting

Management accounting *is the process of identifying, measuring, accumulating, analyzing, preparing, interpreting, and communicating financial information to enable managers to plan, evaluate, and control an organization. For this purpose, management accounting can use a variety of financial and nonmonetary data (Shim and Siegel 2000).*

Cost accounting *focuses specifically on cost information: cost recording and reporting, cost measurement, cost management, and cost analysis. Cost management is obtaining product- or service-costing data and using that information to help managers make decisions related to the products and services in question (pricing, technology, and so on). Cost analysis involves critically examining cost data and translating them into useful information for managerial planning, control, and decision making (see table 4.1).*

4.1. Objectives of management and cost accounting

What motivates management and cost accounting? The information provided in the companywide financial accounts used to issue the statutory accounts reviewed in chapter 3 is not sufficient for managers to conduct operations effectively, tactically, and strategically. They also need external market information—about competitors and the economic, political, and social environments. In addition, they need detailed internal information.

To guide decisions such as pricing, managers will want to know various costs, such as the cost of a specific product or service, a unit within the company, or a

Table 4.1. Differences between financial accounting and cost analysis

Financial accounting	Cost analysis
Provides data for external users.	Provides data for internal users.
Subject to generally accepted accounting principles.	Not subject to generally accepted accounting principles.
Emphasizes accurate and timely data.	Emphasizes relevance and flexibility of data.
Focuses on the business as a whole.	Focuses on parts as well as on the whole of a business.
Primarily stands by itself.	Draws heavily from other disciplines such as finance, economics, and quantitative methods.
Is an end in itself.	Is a means to an end.

Source: Shim and Siegel 2000.

project; or the cost of supplying a customer or a specific group or category of customers. In short, managers will want to know the cost of whatever they decide to analyze.

To conduct any reporting or profitability analysis or any cost control, managers have to rely on a cost accounting system. More specifically, they need to undertake cost analysis and to allocate costs to specific objectives that they define. Cost objectives can be

- geographically oriented—that is, oriented to a specific country or region, or to a specific sales location;
- customer oriented—that is, oriented to specific categories of customers classified by wealth, way of life, consumption behavior, age, ethnic group, or other characteristics;
- product or service oriented—that is, oriented to a specific product (service) or line of products (services);
- plant oriented; or
- business unit oriented.

Profitability analysis and price determination are obvious goals of cost accounting systems and cost allocation processes, but they are not the only goals. Managers can also use them for motivation (see box 4.1); as a basis for cost reimbursement (a condition of some contracts or controls in sectors such as defense contracting, health care, and public utilities); or for income and asset measurement for external

> **Box 4.1. Use of cost accounting and cost allocation systems for motivation**
>
> Cost allocation can be used to serve management goals by encouraging or discouraging departments to use specific services. Management is concerned that the marketing department is not using the services of the legal department. This practice has caused legal problems with corporate communication. In addition to some specific collaboration procedures, management could use cost allocation as an incentive for the marketing department to use those legal services. It could allocate a portion of the costs of the legal department to the marketing department. Because the marketing department will have to pay for these services anyway, the manager will be more willing to use these services. Now assume that the company's design department uses the services of the legal department too intensively, because the costs are not properly allocated to that department. The company's general management can then decide to implement a higher allocation of costs or an allocation based on research and consultation hours, to remind the design department to use the services more effectively.
>
> *Source:* Authors.

4

parties (stockholders or tax administrations). This chapter discusses the principles that management can apply when using the cost accounting and cost allocation systems.

4.2. Cost classifications

Cost classifications are essential to any cost analysis. Many types of cost classifications can be used, depending on managers' analytical needs of management. The four main types of cost classifications used by managers are

- management function (manufacturing and nonmanufacturing costs);
- degree of averaging (total and average cost);
- timing of charges against sales (period and product costs); and
- relevance to planning, control, and decision making.

The last type can be divided into costs by behavior (variable and fixed costs, direct and indirect costs) and "other."

Management function

Management function costs are divided according to the associated functional activities: manufacturing costs and nonmanufacturing costs.

Manufacturing costs

Manufacturing costs are related to the production process of the company and include direct materials, direct labor, and manufacturing overheads.

- *Direct materials* (or raw materials) are materials that become an integral part of the company's finished product. The term *direct* implies easy tracing. Other materials (normally referred to as *indirect* materials) are not easily traced and so are considered part of manufacturing overheads (for example, lubricants and cleaning supplies).
- *Direct labor* is related to the physical labor force used directly in making products in a "hands-on" sense. In furniture making, for example, a carpenter's wage can be considered a direct labor cost.
- *Manufacturing overheads* are all manufacturing costs except direct materials and direct labor: indirect materials costs; indirect labor costs such as wages of factory supervisory personnel; and all other costs relating to the manufacturing division, such as depreciation of factory buildings and equipment, factory utilities, and insurances related to the manufacturing activity.

Nonmanufacturing costs

Nonmanufacturing costs or operating expenses are related to marketing or selling and administrative expenses that cannot be traced during the manufacturing process. Legal expenses or executive compensation are examples of nonmanufacturing costs.

Degree of averaging

Knowing the average cost per unit of a product or service is useful for internal reporting and pricing purposes or for comparing costs among firms. Average unit cost is simply the total cost divided by an appropriate denominator, which is selected on the basis of specific needs, such as unit price per product or unit cost per client. Average cost can be easily related to pricing issues. In competitive markets, a firm will maximize its profit when price equals marginal costs. In the case of natural monopolies (such as public utilities), however, setting prices at marginal cost would lead to problems of sustainability, because the firm would not cover its fixed costs (average cost is greater than marginal cost).

Timing of charges against revenue

The timing of charges against revenue concerns the relation of costs to the manufacturing of a product. On this basis, costs can be classified as *product costs* (or *inventoriable costs*) or *period costs*.

Product costs are treated as inventory until the product is sold, which may not be in the production period that the cost was incurred. When the product is sold, the costs become expenses—costs of goods sold. This means that these costs are initially in the balance sheet as assets (unsold merchandise) and that they move into the income statement when they become expenses (when the unit is sold). Typically, raw material costs are product costs.

Period costs are always incurred in a single period and so do not go through an inventory stage. Items such as sales commission, office rent, and other nonmanufacturing costs are examples of period costs. More generally, all sales and administrative expenses are period costs.

Relevance to planning, control, and decision making

Costs relevant to planning, control, and decision making can be classified by cost behavior and other characteristics.

Cost classification by behavior

Classifying costs by behavior—by how costs respond to changes in the level of the business activity—is essential for understanding cost allocation. The most common cost behaviors under scrutiny are *variable and fixed costs* and *direct and indirect costs*.

Variable and fixed costs. The typology of variable and fixed costs classifies costs according to their behavior when changes occur in the business activity. If activity rises or falls, some costs move along with the level of activity, while others remain constant.

Variable costs vary with the level of business activity, but not all variable costs have the same behavior pattern. Some behave in a proportionately variable pattern, whereas others behave in a step-variable pattern and might not change with small increases in the level of production. An example of *true variable costs* is direct materials. Whatever the increase in production, materials will need to increase proportionately, so more costs are associated with production. An example of *step-variable costs* is the labor costs of maintenance workers. Their workload might not change with nonsubstantial increases or decreases in production.

Fixed costs remain constant in total, regardless of the level of activity within the relevant range. As a result, fixed costs are not affected by changes in activity during a period. Examples of fixed costs are rents, research costs, advertising costs, depreciation of buildings and equipment, and salaries of operating personnel. Fixed costs are sometimes referred to as *capacity costs*, because they are related to expenses incurred for plant facilities, equipment, and other items needed to provide the basic capacity to satisfy customers' demands.

Because fixed costs are constant over a range of activities, unit cost declines as volume increases, while variable costs remain the same (because raising production also raises variable costs so that the unit variable cost is unchanged). Hence the concept of "variable and fixed" refers to the cost rather than the units (table 4.2). Considering total costs divided by total volume without distinguishing fixed and variable costs can lead to misleading interpretations.

Direct and indirect costs. *Direct costs* are costs that can be directly traceable to a specific activity (a cost objective). Direct costs do not cause problems of allocation, because they are easily allocated to a specific activity. Materials and labor directly used when producing a specific good or delivering a specific service are direct costs.

Table 4.2. Cost behavior—Fixed and variable costs

Cost type	Cost behavior	
	In total	Per unit
Variable cost	Increases and decreases in proportion to changes in the level of activity	Remains constant per unit
Fixed cost	Unaffected by changes in the level of activity	Decreases per unit as the level of activity rises and increases per unit as the level of activity falls

Source: Authors.

The cost of the fuel used by a generator and the salaries of the technicians in charge of that generator are direct costs of energy generation, for example.

Indirect costs are costs that cannot be assigned directly to a specific product or service. As will be seen in the discussion of cost allocation issues, indirect costs can give rise to problems, because they need to be assigned to the different products and services provided by the company. Examples of indirect costs are marketing and advertising costs, top management costs, indirect factory-labor costs, and depreciation of buildings. Indirect costs are also called *common costs* or *joint costs*, between which a subtle difference exists.

Joint costs arise when a single and indivisible process gives rise to several products or services. An example of a joint cost is the cost of cattle for producing hides and beef (one cow less or more means a reduction or increase in the same proportion of hides and beef). Another example is the cost of a cotton field to produce cottonseed and cotton fiber.

Common costs arise when a single process gives rise to several products or services, even though they can be produced separately. For example, the cost of equipment that can be used to produce two products is a common cost. Unlike joint costs, common costs can vary to some degree with the quantity of production of each product, even though they are not directly attributable to a single product. With joint costs, variation in production of one product necessitates simultaneous variation in production of the other product. When allocating costs, tracing common costs back to units of a specific output (product or service) is usually easier than tracing joint costs because of this relative variability characteristic.

Cost typologies unrelated to behavior
Other cost typologies not related to cost behavior but also relevant to planning, control, and decision making are

- controllable and uncontrollable costs,
- opportunity costs,
- sunk costs,
- incremental (or differential) costs and marginal costs, and
- stand-alone costs.

Controllable and uncontrollable costs. A cost is considered controllable at a specific level of an organization if it is significantly under the influence of the managers at that level. Controllability can be linked to the organization of the entity (does the manager have the authority to authorize the cost in question?). It can also be related to the price of the good or service. For example, if fuel is necessary to produce the good or service, it can be considered an uncontrollable cost, because its price is fixed on the international market.[1] Controllability also includes a time dimension. Costs that are controllable over the long term may not be controllable over the short term.

Opportunity costs. An opportunity cost is the net benefit forgone by choosing one alternative over others. Opportunity costs are not entered on the accounting books of a company.

Sunk costs. A sunk cost is a cost that has already been incurred and cannot be changed by any decision made now or in the future. Sunk costs should be considered irrelevant to future decisions.

Incremental (or differential) costs and marginal costs. Accountants understand incremental or differential cost as the cost difference between two alternatives. More accurately, differential costs are either incremental (increase in cost from one alternative to another) or decremental (decrease in cost from one alternative to another). Differential costs can be variable or fixed.

The accountant's concept of differential cost can be compared with the economist's concept of marginal cost, as can their views of incremental cost. Marginal costs are relative to the costs of producing one additional unit of output. For economists, setting prices at marginal costs leads to optimal use of resources and send true signals of costs to customers.

The activities for which companies can plan additional single units of output are few. Rather, companies prefer to plan in blocks or increments of output. In practice, incremental costs are used more than marginal costs. An increment of output could be generated solely by a new activity that a company would like to undertake. The incremental cost would then refer to the specific costs of that new activity. Incremental costing methods are used in pricing decisions and control, but further discussion is beyond the scope of this volume (for more detail, see Munasinghe 1990a and 1990b).

Stand-alone costs. When a company has several activities, the stand-alone cost of a specific activity is the cost that would be incurred if the company undertook solely that activity.

Comparison of cost classifications

Figure 4.1 illustrates the main approaches to cost classifications for a company that manufactures and markets its own products. Product costs are manufacturing costs, and period costs are nonmanufacturing costs. Direct labor and direct materials costs are variable costs. Other manufacturing costs can be variable (materials not directly traceable to a product) or fixed (rent or depreciation of factory building). Most nonmanufacturing costs are fixed costs, but some can be variable (such as sales commission). Variable costs such as direct labor or direct materials are direct costs, but all other manufacturing costs not directly traceable to a product are indirect by nature. All nonmanufacturing costs are indirect.

Adding *incremental* and *stand-alone* costs to figure 4.1 would require splitting the indirect costs into common costs and joint costs. About a company that has two activities, A and B, it could be observed that the

Incremental cost of A = all direct costs of A + % common costs of A and B.[2]

Stand-alone costs of A = all direct costs of A + all joint costs of A and B + % common costs of A and B.

Figure 4.1. Comparison of cost classifications

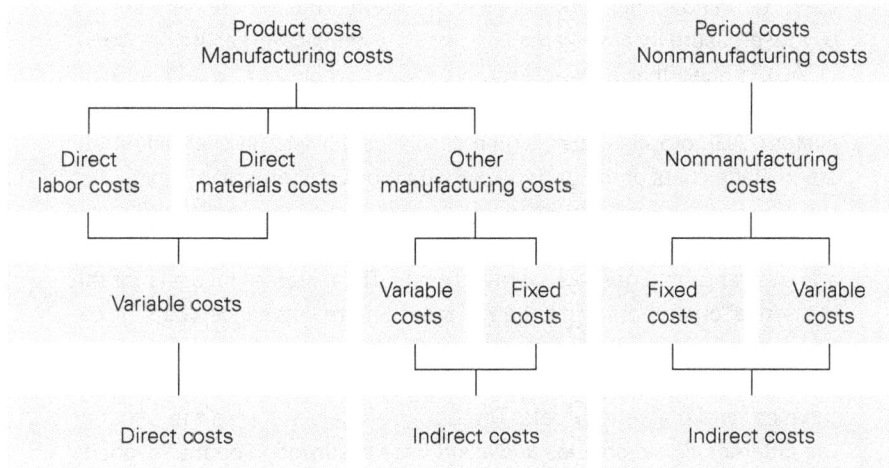

Source: Authors.

When estimating the stand-alone cost of activity A (if the company were hypothetically considering to undertake only that activity), all the joint costs incurred by the company in real life when activities A and B are performed would be included. The logic is that these joint costs (because of their nature) will have to be borne, even if the company decides to perform only activity A. In the example of the cotton field used to produce cottonseed and cotton fiber, the cost of the cotton field will have to be borne, even if the farmer decides to produce only cottonseed and not cotton fiber. However, some of the common costs, such as the administration costs, could probably be cut back if the farmer decides to drop cotton fiber production. Thus only a percentage of the common costs are considered.

Box 4.2 provides an example of stand-alone and incremental pricing.

**Box 4.2. Stand-alone and incremental pricing:
The case of the Australian Gas Light Company**

In its submission to the Independent Pricing and Regulatory Tribunal's (IPART) 1999 access review, the Australian Gas Light Company (AGL) argued that it had rebuilt the gas network mainly on the basis of large users' demand for high-pressure gas. Residential customers were served by low-pressure local systems connected to the high-pressure network.

AGL argued that a low-pressure network would not have been economical if it had to bear the fully distributed cost of the high-pressure system. AGL proposed that high-pressure customers be charged on the stand-alone costs of the network serving those customers, meaning that the high-pressure customers would bear almost all the capital and maintenance costs of the high-pressure network and a larger share of the administrative and general overhead costs. The incremental costs for the residential customers were the full asset and maintenance costs of the low-pressure system, marketing costs, and the additional administrative and general overhead costs resulting from the incremental asset, maintenance, and marketing costs. The box table below shows the effect of the different allocation rules and asset base assumption on the revenues from the contract (high-pressure) customers.

(continues)

Management and Cost Accounting

4.3. Cost allocation

Cost allocation is based on the classification of costs into direct costs and indirect costs, as noted above. The principle of *causality* intrinsic to that classification is a guiding principle of cost allocation.

Cost analysis requires defining the *objective* of that analysis in relation to a manager's goals: the cost objective as introduced in this chapter's first section. Costs have to be assigned to that cost objective. In most cases that means total costs, both direct and indirect. Direct costs cause no allocation problem, because they can be readily traced to a specific cost objective. The difficulty arises with indirect costs. Thus the definition of cost allocation is the assignment and reassignment of indirect costs or groups of indirect costs to one or more cost objectives.

Box 4.2. *(continued)*

Revenue scenarios for contract customers under different asset base and cost allocation methodologies
(millions of Australian dollars)

	Asset valuation methodology			
	ORC	DORC	ICB	DAC
Scenario 1				
Stand-alone allocation of capital and operating costs	$59m	$61m	$52m	$47m
Scenario 2				
Stand-alone allocation of capital cost and fully distributed allocation of operating costs	$58m	$50m	$41m	$36m
Scenario 3				
Fully distributed allocation of capital and operating costs	$53m	$46m	$38m	$34m
AGL's proposal	**$70m**			

Note:
1. Capital costs include return on capital base and depreciation.
2. Return on assets is based on a pre-tax rate of return of 7.75 percent for the scenarios of ORC, DORC, and ICB. A nominal return of 10.44 percent is assumed for the scenario of DAC.
3. Depreciation is assumed to be 2 percent per annum.

IPART rejected the proposal to use the stand-alone/incremental cost allocation. It considered that, given the market's development since the initial investment, a fully distributed cost allocation represented a reasonable balance of the various consumers' interests.

Source: Authors.

The classification of costs and the complexity of the cost allocation process are influenced by the definition of the cost objective. For example, if cost objectives are defined in terms of organizational levels (company, departments, subdepartments, and so on) and if the whole company is the cost objective, all costs would be direct costs. The more objectives are disaggregated or defined finely, the more likely it is that costs will be common to more than one objective.

Goals of cost allocation

The goals of cost allocation are price determination, evaluation of performance and profitability, cost reimbursement, and incentives to use specific services within a company more or less intensively.

General criteria for cost allocation

Depending on their goals, managers can apply different criteria to define their general approach to cost allocation. Four basic criteria can guide their cost allocation decisions:

- *Cause-effect relationship* (*causality principle*). Costs may be allocated on the basis of services provided (costs are allocated to the source that caused the costs to be incurred).
- *Benefits received*. Costs may be allocated on the basis of benefits received (for example, advertising costs might be allocated to products or services of a company on the basis of respective sales).
- *Ability to bear*. Costs may be allocated on the basis of the cost objective's capacity to bear them (for example, higher shares of corporate executives' salaries may be allocated to the most profitable departments or products).
- *Arbitrary allocation*. Costs may be allocated arbitrarily on a lump-sum basis.

The cost allocation choice has to be guided by the dominant goal to be served. For example, causality should be the guiding principle when the decision maker wants to ensure that the price of a good or a service reflects its costs (a main concern to competition or regulatory authorities). But decision makers might choose other principles in some situations. Even regulators sometimes apply a concept similar to ability to bear ("single till" concept). Arbitrary allocation might make sense when managers want to encourage or discourage the use of some services, as noted above. Whatever principle is followed, cost allocation should be straightforward, transparent, and consistent over some time.

A step-by-step process

Cost allocation is basically a step-by-step process that requires identifying and classifying costs as direct or indirect, tracing direct costs to the cost objectives, grouping indirect costs in cost pools, and allocating the cost pools to the cost objectives. Figure 4.2 summarizes a general cost allocation process.

Cost allocation entails five steps:

1. Choosing a cost objective
2. Identifying direct costs and tracing them to cost objectives
3. Pooling (choosing and accumulating in pools) the remaining indirect costs that relate to the cost objective defined in step 1
4. Choosing a method of relating the indirect costs in step 3 to the cost objective in step 1—choosing a cost allocation base
5. Assigning direct and indirect costs to cost objectives

Following this process, all costs will be *allocated* or *distributed*.

Choosing a cost objective

The first step in a cost allocation process is identifying what to study. Cost objectives can be a product or a service; a department or division of the company; a production

Figure 4.2. General cost allocation process

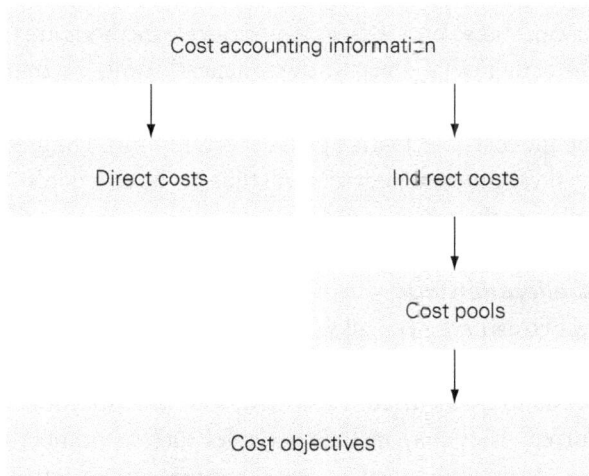

Source: Authors.

process, a specific job, contract, or customer; a sales region; or an organizational segment.

Identifying direct costs and tracing them to cost objectives

Identifying costs that are directly traceable to a specific cost objective causes no allocation problems.[3] Relevant here is another type of basic cost classification—that involving fixed costs and variable costs. Recall that all direct costs are variable costs (direct costs will vary in total in proportion to fluctuations in the level of service consumed), but all variable costs are not direct costs (see table 4.2).

Pooling indirect costs that relate to cost objectives

Costs that cannot be directly traceable to a specific cost objective are the remaining indirect costs (common costs or joint costs). Cost allocation thus refers to the allocation of these indirect costs. The individual indirect cost items that relate to the cost objective have to be identified and then regrouped into homogeneous cost pools. A cost pool is homogeneous when the activity for which costs are included have a cause-effect relationship to the cost objective defined, as have other activities for which costs are included in that cost pool. Such homogeneity facilitates application of a single cost driver in allocating the cost pool to final cost objectives.

The number of cost pools depends on the number of cost groups that are identified and on the relative importance of the different cost items. In simple allocation methods, cost pools can simply be departments of the company (personnel, purchasing, production, and so on). *Activity-based costing* methods are more complex. They identify the activities (actions, work sequences, events, or transactions) that cause an indirect cost to be incurred in production of the product or provision of the service (when the cost objective is a product or a service). The groups of indirect costs allocated to these different activities will thus be the cost pools. Then the main issue is how to allocate these cost pools.

Choosing a cost allocation base

Once the indirect costs have been allocated to multiple cost pools, the cost pools must be assigned to the cost objectives through the allocation bases or cost drivers that cause the costs to be incurred. Cost drivers are activity measures that cause costs to be incurred. They may include variables such as number of employees, labor hours, area of space occupied, or any other measure of activity in a department. Ideally, the base has some cause-and-effect relationship with the cost.

Basically, cost drivers can be divided into three types:

- *Input based*. Allocation is based on the share of the other attributable inputs (direct labor, direct materials, and so on).
- *Output based*. Allocation is based on output indicators such as the production or sales volume share of the given product in total output of the company.
- *Revenue based*. Allocation is based on revenues generated by the product in question.

Cost allocation influences the choice of cost driver. Revenue-based cost drivers, for example, are inconsistent with the principle of causality. They do not take into account the specific technology or processes used in production of a good or delivery of a service. They simply assume that the more (or less) revenues a product or service generates the more (or less) costs are incurred.

In all cases, the choice of cost drivers has to be motivated by *cost of measurement* and *degree of correlation*. With respect to the former, information for the chosen cost driver must be available at reasonable cost. If machine-hours appears to be an appropriate cost driver, information has to be available for the machine. If not, the manager must figure out the cost of generating the information. With respect to degree of correlation, a consistent relationship between the cost driver and the consumption of the item in question must be known.

Assigning direct and indirect costs to cost objects

Eventually, all identified direct costs and allocated indirect costs will be assigned to cost objectives.

Cost allocation approaches and methods

Costs can be allocated following an accounting approach or an economic approach.

Accounting approaches

Two basic accounting approaches to cost allocation are fully distributed costs and activity-based costs.

Fully distributed costs. The fully distributed cost (FDC) approach is the general accounting approach to cost allocation. It follows the general step-by-step approach described in the third main section of this chapter.

The FDC approach allocates all costs among cost objectives on the basis of the principle of causality but uses imprecise cost drivers, such as a broad volume-based driver (number of units sold) or value-based drivers (sales).

The main criticisms of FDC are related to the arbitrary cost allocation (based on a simple ratio) and lack of economic efficiency. Economists have also criticized use of the FDC approach to test for cross-subsidies between services.

The lower limit and upper limit of subsidy-free prices are the incremental cost and the stand-alone cost, respectively. To understand these limits, assume two cost objectives, A and B. Segment the indirect costs of A and B into common costs and joint costs. The FDC approach simply allocates a share of the common costs *and* joint costs to cost objectives A and B. Incremental costing views one objective, A for example, as the primary objective and the other, B, as the incremental objective. Therefore, one part of the common costs are allocated to the incremental part B, but none of the joint costs (as these expenses are incurred anyway by the primary objective). In stand-alone costing of B, the process is the same, but all joint costs are allocated to B (as explained in 4.2, this chapter).

Incremental cost of B = all direct costs of B + % common costs of A and B.

**Stand-alone costs of B = all direct costs of B + all joint costs of A and B
+ % common costs of A and B.**

Therefore, stand-alone costs and incremental costs can be used as upper and lower limits of the FDC approach to test the relevance of the approach's estimations.

These costing approaches are common in pricing issues and occasion considerable discussion in competition and regulatory debates. In a common example, company X accuses competitor Y of predatory pricing when launching a new product or service. In making its argument, company Y uses the incremental costing approach to validate its price for the new product or service, and company X challenges the estimation on the basis of fully distributed cost, which results in a higher cost.

The FDC method allocates all costs, both direct and indirect, to the cost objectives. The time horizon and the nature of decisions might lead managers to choose a different method. For example, when considering short-term decisions to maximize the use of various organizational segments' existing capacity, managers are not interested in FDCs to the segments, because they will not be able to influence the common fixed costs in the short term. Managers will only be interested in the

4

direct variable costs of each organizational segment. They will compare these costs with the revenues that each segment can generate. When confronted with the choice of using existing capacity in plant A or installing new capacity in plant B, managers will be better off using plant A as long as the plant's incremental costs are lower than the cost of installing and running new capacity in plant B. The FDCs of plant B may be lower than those of plant A, but this information is not relevant to the decision as long as sufficient spare capacity exists in plant A.

Activity-based costing. The activity-based costing method (sometimes called transaction costing) is considered more accurate than the FDC method in allocating indirect costs such as manufacturing overheads. Activity-based costing focuses on processes or activities rather than final goods or services outputs. It links costs to these processes and then links these processes back to final goods or services outputs.

Garrison and Noreen (1994) note that activity-based costing improves costing systems in three ways:

- It increases the number of cost pools used to accumulate indirect costs such as overhead costs. Rather than accumulate all the costs simply—for example, in company department pools—costs are accumulated by activity.
- It changes the bases used to assign indirect costs to products. Rather than assigning costs on the basis of a simple measure such as volume, costs are assigned on the basis of the activities that generate the costs.
- It changes the nature of many indirect costs, reclassifying them into direct costs so that they can be traced to specific activities.

Activity-based costing attempts to capture the intrinsic "technology" of production or service delivered through managers' understanding of the different processes and activities involved. It requires a deep knowledge of the company's activities. The drawback of this approach is that if technology changes—if the relationship between inputs and final products and services through processes and activities changes—the allocation method has to change too.

Economic approach to allocation: Ramsey pricing

Economic approaches to cost allocation such as the Ramsey approach are based on demand factors rather than cause-effect relationships. The Ramsey approach consists of allocating common costs on the basis of the price elasticity of demand for each service. Cost allocation is inversely proportional to elasticity, and thus a bigger share of cost is allocated to activities or products that are less sensitive to price variations. From an economic point of view, this allocation rule is optimal, because the deviation of prices from their marginal costs will have a smaller effect on real resource flows. Put another way, the actual resource flows would be closer to those that would occur if all prices were set at their marginal costs. However, this approach is difficult to put into practice, because demand elasticities are not always easy to estimate.[4]

Cost distortion or cross-subsidization

When costs are not appropriately assigned to cost objectives, cross-subsidies and distortions occur. The activity to which some of its own costs were not assigned will be subsidized by the activities to which these costs were improperly assigned. The subsidization will lead managers to make the wrong decisions for the given activities on the basis of profitability analyses and price determination studies. This concept is important for regulators.

Cross-subsidization may occur when companies

- fail to trace costs directly to the segments when the situation requires it,
- use inappropriate bases to allocate costs, or
- arbitrarily allocate common costs to segments.

Chapters 5 and 6 show that cross-subsidization is a central concern in regulation. One of the main roles of regulators is to avoid unfair cross-subsidization between or among different classes of customers or cross-subsidization of a competitive service by a noncompetitive service that creates "undue" discrimination. Cross-subsidies, when allowed by regulators, should be quantified and transparent, and the reason for them should be clearly stated. An example is a decision to subsidize tariffs for low-income customers through low tariffs on low consumption levels. The regulator should consider whether other policy instruments (for example, direct transfers) would be a better means of achieving stated objectives.

Allocate budgeted costs or actual costs?

Whether indirect costs are allocated to cost objectives on an actual basis or on a budgeted basis has implications for efficiency.

Consider a company that wants to allocate the costs of a service department (say, marketing) to operating units. The choice of method has consequence for the manager's cost and profitability analysis. If actual costs are allocated without proper cost control, any management efficiency of the service department will be hidden in the routine allocation of the cost of that department to the operating units. If allocation is made on the basis of budgeted costs, which are calculated on an efficiency basis, any possible inefficiency will be retained in the service department and not passed on to operating units.[5]

Additional reading and resources

Horngren, C. T., and G. Foster. 1987. *Cost Accounting: A Managerial Emphasis*. 6th ed. Upper Saddle River, NJ: Prentice Hall.

Garrison, R. H., and E. W. Noreen. 1994. *Managerial Accounting*. Burr Ridge, IL: Irwin

Oxera. 2003. "Assessing Profitability in Competition Policy Analysis." Economic Discussion Paper 6. Prepared for the UK Office of Fair Trading, London. (See part I, section 6, on cost and revenue allocation.)

Shim, J. K., and J. G. Siegel. 2000. *Modern Cost Management and Analysis*. 2nd ed. New York: Barron's Business Library.

4

Notes

1. Nonetheless, the manager is responsible for rationalizing its use in the production process. This specific cost typology is examined again in chapter 6.

2. In the extreme, a company can decide to put to "0" the percentage of common costs, meaning that all common costs are allocated to activity B.

3. Revenues should not pose a problem, because they, too, can be easily traced to a specific activity. Problems might arise with revenues streaming from joint products (a "sales package" with one price for two combined products).

4. Under a regulatory perspective, fairness is always stated as an argument against the Ramsey rule.

5. Managers will have to compare budgeted costs with actual costs to identify the variance, which they will have to explain and remedy.

Chapter 5

Why Do Regulatory Accounting?

In the same way that managers of a company rely on cost accounting in making their planning and control decisions, regulators rely on cost accounting in making decisions related to their regulatory responsibilities. When a company supplies more than one product or service, managers and regulators need to relate the price of each product and service to its costs. They need to estimate the cash flow generated by each product or service and the value of the assets required by each activity. They use this information to calculate the internal rate of return of the activity and to compare it to its cost of capital.[1] Then managers can determine whether developing that activity is worthwhile, and regulators and competition agencies can detect excessive or insufficient profits.

Managers and regulators rely on the same basic financial indicators to measure the profitability of an activity, but regulators have different and wider objectives than managers, so they need management accounting formatted to those objectives. Regulators need to define their specific cost objectives and their own allocation rules and methodologies. Like managers, regulators use the company's information to guide the setting of prices (tariffs) of the products and services sold by the company.[2]

Regulators also have to deal with monopolies or significant market power situations, usually associated with utilities or other network industries such as transport. These specific needs require specific accounting arrangements: regulatory accounting. Because of these specific market situations, regulators have to ensure that prices are fair and reasonable and that they reflect efficient costs. Therefore, regulators are particularly concerned with issues such as cross-subsidization and economic and efficient management.

Chapter 3 introduced cross-subsidization (or cost distortion). This chapter and chapter 6 examine the specific impact of this concern on the organization of accounting.

5.1. Regulatory accounting and its objectives

Regulatory accounting is a set of principles and rules of presentation of information for regulated companies. These rules enable an allocation of companies' costs, revenues, assets, and liabilities in a way that facilitates control of the regulatory objectives.

The practical objective of regulatory accounting arrangements is to provide information to assist regulators in dealing with the particular market situation of utilities and transport. This information should allow regulators to verify compliance with the basic regulatory objectives that were defined in chapter 1: sustainability, allocative efficiency, productive efficiency, and equity (or distributive efficiency).

The principles underlying implementation of regulatory accounting are strongly related to these four basic objectives. Most legal texts or guidelines related to the regulatory framework state the rationale for regulation in the following terms:

- Monitor performance against the assumptions underlying price controls.
- Detect anticompetitive behavior (for example, unfair cross-subsidization and undue discrimination).
- Assist in monitoring the financial health of the operator.
- Set prices.

Regulators have to make trade-offs among these objectives. In prioritizing objectives, regulators need to consider the intrinsic characteristics of the industry network they regulate (the degree of competition, the amount and type of investments needed); the economic, social, and political environment of the country; and so on. In network industries such as electricity and water, the main focus is often on monitoring performance, setting fair and reasonable prices, and ensuring that prices reflect efficiency costs.[3] In telecommunications, the major preoccupation is often detecting anticompetitive behavior, such as cross-subsidization and undue discrimination.[4]

In addition, regulatory accounting arrangements serve three practical objectives:

- They assist in benchmarking and in comparative competition (by promoting the submission of comparable information by the different companies regulated by the same authority).

- They improve transparency (and help all parties understand the regulatory authority's information requirements and regulatory functions) and reduce regulatory risk.
- They ensure that regulated companies report to the regulatory authority on a timely, consistent, structured, and accurate basis.

A different presentation of data is not the only way cost accounting used by companies differs from regulatory accounting, however. While facing some important restrictions in assuming this exercise, regulators should also have the right to reject some costs judged to be "imprudent" or "inefficient." Costs should not be excluded lightly, but the right to exclude them in some circumstances is a common element in regulation. Therefore, in the definition of regulatory accounting, *allocation of cost* is understood to mean the *allocation of prudent and efficient costs.*

5.2. General presentation of information needs

This section introduces information needs in a general way by presenting the main elements for defining that information. Chapter 6 details some key issues, such as segmentation of activities, determination of the regulatory asset base and its depreciation, and disclosure of information linked to related-party transactions.

Basically, regulators have to define their information needs in terms of the

- *perimeter of the information*, such as the overall coverage of the regulated activities to be reported, separation of information on subactivities, and disclosure of information on unregulated activities;
- *content of the information*, both financial and nonfinancial;
- *format of the information*, such as the classification of accounts and appropriate level of disaggregation; and
- *periodicity of reporting*, depending on the nature of the information and of the operator's obligations.

Regulators also have to define their own *allocation and valuation rules.*

Perimeter of information

Regulators have to define the perimeter of information they will need to verify compliance with regulatory objectives. The perimeter of information includes most data of the regulated companies, which are required to separate regulated activities from unregulated activities. In addition, companies are usually required to segment the regulated activities into subactivities, such as production, transport, and distribution.

The allocation and segmentation of costs enables the regulator to check for unfair cross-subsidization and undue discrimination (see chapter 6, on separation of activities). The financial data on unregulated activities need to be delivered to the regulator to enable reconciliation with standard statutory accounts and to facilitate the check for unfair cross-subsidization.

The regulator might not use only the financial (accounting) information received from the operator to determine tariffs. The regulator's role is also to ensure that the costs used to set up future tariffs are "efficient" costs (see the discussion below).

The regulator requires nonfinancial data related to the company's regulated operations to monitor the operator's efficiency. Although treatment of the information needs related to nonfinancial data is beyond the scope of this chapter, several points are worth mentioning here. First, the regulator needs to be able to match financial and nonfinancial data on a common basis. Therefore, the cost and revenue separation imposed on the regulatory accounting has to be compatible with the disaggregation of the nonfinancial data (for example, number of employees and time devoted to each activity). Second, in many cases nonfinancial data will be useful in defining and checking the criteria for allocations among activities. A common and consistent framework for treating financial data and nonfinancial data is thus crucial.

Content of information

Regulators, to meet their objectives, have to specify the information to be provided to them: financial information (balance sheets, profit and loss accounts, cash flow statements, and so on) and nonfinancial information (economic, environmental, users' consumption, technical indicators related to efficiency and quality, and so on). Specifying the content is a key requirement. Information reported by companies using standard statements does not allow the regulator to verify compliance with regulatory objectives.

Format of information

Regulators must specify not only the content, but also the format of the financial and nonfinancial information. For example, regulators need to define the classification of accounts and the appropriate level of disaggregation of the chart of accounts for all relevant financial statements.[5]

Periodicity of reporting

Regulators have to specify the periodicity of information to be provided. The periodicity is based on the nature of the information and of the operator's obligations (investments).

For general financial information, annual or biannual periodicity might be appropriate. But regulators may require shorter periodicity—often quarterly reporting—for primary technical and efficiency indicators (such as interruption of service) and for capital expenditures.[6] For some critical variables, monthly reporting may be required. The key issue is to detect efficiency problems or failure of compliance with an investment obligation as early as possible. For services that show a seasonal pattern (in demand or cost conditions), more detailed information might be used for properly allocating costs (peak-load pricing).

Service interruptions or efficiency problems send negative signals about operation of the service. Their cause should be analyzed as soon as possible to rectify the situation and to reduce any further occurrence. Failure to meet investment obligations or forecast capital expenditure is a more delicate situation. It may reflect changes in circumstances (such as slower-than-expected demand growth) or efficiency improvements by the operator. If the company has no justification for its lack of investment, the regulator may act to "recuperate" the amount of unmet investment obligation through reduced future tariffs (after interaction with the operator and process of dispute and arbitrage if necessary).[7] In practice, however, this situation is complex to analyze and becomes even more so if handled a year later because of the particular periodicity of reporting.

The regulator also needs to consider carefully the impact of such steps on incentives. If the regulator penalizes the operator—deliberate unmotivated noncompliance is rare—it will not encourage the operator to seek future efficiency and cost reductions relative to the original contractual investment plan. To avoid problems, the operator will simply incur the forecast expenses instead.

Detecting and dealing with noncompliance as soon as possible is preferable to avoid more difficult conflicts and legal procedures.

Allocation and valuation rules

Regulators usually define general allocation and valuation principles such as the following:

- *Causality*. Costs, revenues, and capital employed should be allocated to the activities (services offered or user category served by the regulated company) that incur the costs or revenues.
- *Objectivity*. Allocation and valuation methodologies should be designed on an objective basis and not in a way that unfairly benefits the regulated company or any other party.
- *Consistency*. Allocation criteria should remain the same over time, to the extent that is feasible and reasonable.
- *Transparency*. Allocation methodologies should be clear, and the various included parts of the costs should be clearly differentiated from one another.

The spirit of these principles is similar to that underlying the generally accepted accounting principles (GAAP) for statutory accounts and the principles used as cost allocation guidelines in cost accounting, though GAAP do not strictly apply to cost analysis (see chapter 3) and regulatory accounting requirements can differ from GAAP.

The principles and rules for valuation methodologies will usually be detailed. Valuation of assets is central to regulation, because one of the main cost elements that will determine the revenues allowed to the operator is the authorized return on these assets. (Valuation methodologies are detailed in chapter 6.)

5.3. Limitations of traditional and management accounting of the regulated company

The information provided by traditional financial accounting does not meet the needs of regulators for two primary reasons. First, costs cannot be separated by regulated and unregulated activities. Second, regulators need historical data to forecast costs and revenues for future tariff setting.[8]

Moreover, if regulators rely only on statutory financial statements, they will have only very limited ability to compare operators because of the heterogeneity of information reporting.

Can regulators use the information provided by management accounting and implemented by the company? The answer is not obvious, because of several limitations:

- The cost and managerial accounting system was put in place to meet the specific objectives of the company's managers. Regulators do not have the same objectives. Thus the specific needs of the regulator and a cost accounting plan will have to be defined in accordance with these objectives.
- The information in a cost and managerial accounting system is usually considered internal "confidential" information. Thus information exchange procedures and mechanisms will have to be implemented within a legal regulatory framework.
- No standards relating to management accounting exist. For example, in the case of cost analysis and allocation, methodologies might differ from one company to another. Thus, for the regulator to monitor several regulated companies in the same sector and to compare the costs of their services, the companies' cost accounting plans would have to be mutually defined in accordance with these objectives.

5.4. Consistency between statutory accounts and regulatory accounts

The specific needs of regulators and their various objectives will require elaboration of specific regulatory accounting statements, which are defined further in chapters 6 and 7. This section lays out some principles about these statements and how they relate to statutory accounts. Regulatory accounting statements

- are additional to any statutory financial reporting obligations of the companies under the general accounting law;
- must be prepared on the basis of GAAP, unless explicitly specified;
- are based on the same source of information as statutory accounts statements (regulatory accounting statements should always be reconciled with statutory accounts statements); and
- will follow regulatory accounting guidelines over accounting standards wherever the two conflict (see chapter 6).[9]

It must be emphasized that regulators rely on the same sources of information as managers and use data derived from the same information systems. Regulators must ensure that their needs are specified well in advance so that the cost accounting plan and the data recording processes can be defined to follow their information requirements.

5.5. Regulators' behavior and principles to follow

Regulators have to balance the interests of various groups—government, operator, and users—to meet the goal of the public interest. The tension among these interests can be overstated. It is not in consumers' interest, for example, for prices to be below efficient costs, including a commercial rate of return. But day-to-day tensions are part of the regulatory process. Companies will be concerned to ensure that the regulator does not squeeze profits too much or interfere in the running of the business. Customers may have strong expectations that the regulator will squeeze out any cost padding or unfair prices sooner rather than later.

The two extreme positions that a regulator could adopt when monitoring a regulated operator are ignorance and interference.

Ignorance

Ignorance can arise from various situations:

- The operator delivers no information, whether because of shortcomings in the legal framework or the contract, or because the regulator is not sufficiently active in enforcing it.
- The regulator does not use the information provided by the operator appropriately (no rigorous and systematic analytical work).
- The regulator relies too much on the incentive properties of the regulations adopted and is less concerned with price structures or anticompetitive behavior.

Because of the lack of information, the regulator will be unable to verify that the regulatory objectives of sustainability, allocative and productive efficiency, and equity (distributive efficiency) are achieved. Whatever the causes, the government and the regulator should remedy the situation through dialogue with the operator, new decrees or laws addressing the issue, sanctions, or other means.

Interference

Interference or micromanagement refers to regulators' constant questioning of managers' decisions. When regulators behave as though they were part of the company's management, accountabilities are confused and incentives are poor. Such action is detrimental to the interests of all stakeholders. Furthermore, it can undercut the government's policy objectives and intentions for sector reform, because the decision to turn a public utility over to private sector management (management contract, concession) or control (privatization) to improve efficiency and services is being undermined.

Risks

Both ignorance and interference involve risk. The main risk of ignorance is that objectives are not met because of the impossibility of verifying compliance with regulatory objectives. This situation puts the public interest in danger.[10] The main risk of interference is the abuse of regulatory powers and overregulation. By increasing perceived risk in the name of efficiency, interference results in a higher cost of capital required by the operators and, probably, in greater inefficiency.

The regulator has to adopt a responsible position between these two attitudes. Although it appears obvious that a regulator should neither ignore information nor interfere constantly in management of the regulated operator, experience shows that this balance is difficult to achieve. Initially there may be a need to improve information systems, but the tendency to demand more detailed and complex information is strong. Regulators also have to be realistic and adapt their regulatory work to their capacity and competence.

5.6. Using accounting costs in tariff determination

The relationship between an operator's accounting costs and the operator's tariffs depends to a large extent on the regulatory regime and the specific rules of each service. As long as the regulator has a duty toward the economic and financial sustainability of the regulated firm, the operator's costs will be an important element to take into account in a tariff determination. Nevertheless, accounting costs do not necessarily go directly into the determination of tariffs. As much as possible, the rules and criteria to be used by a regulator in reviewing accounting costs should be carefully spelled out in advance. Some general principles, such as a presumption of prudent management, realism, and materiality (discussed below), should guide the regulator. A well-defined sanction still entails risks for the operator; these risks should be factored into the overall regulatory framework and the rewards provided.

Figure 5.1 summarizes a standard process to reach the optimal tariff determination.

Excluding costs

As mentioned in the discussion of the perimeter of information, the original accounting data provided to the regulator by the operator should not necessarily be used as they are for tariff determination (even when correctly allocated). Regulators not only have the right to audit the data (see discussion below), but can exclude some lines of costs or approve only partially incurred expenses. One of the main roles of the regulator is to ensure that companies have an incentive to operate as efficiently as they would in a competitive environment. Inefficient costs should not be recovered from customers through tariffs. The sanction of some inefficient costs—even excluding them completely—can be part of the incentive regime and has parallels with outcomes in unregulated markets.

To avoid unnecessary and inefficient increases in the risks perceived by investors, these cost exclusions should adhere to clear and predictable rules.

The regulator might decide to exclude inefficiently incurred costs in full or in part.[11] Full lines of costs (specific cost items) may be excluded, because they are not considered useful (within a reasonable planning horizon for delivering the regulated service). Even if the cost is conceptually related to the delivery of the regulated service, regulators may partially exclude incurred expenses where they are shown to be clearly inefficient. Regulators want to avoid the risk that the regulated companies incurred expenses at a cost higher than their market value.

If the regulator decides to exclude what are considered *inefficient costs*, regulated operators want to know the legal grounds for this action. In the United States the basic authority for a regulatory agency insisting on prudent costs (including investments) relies on the "just and reasonable" standard. If common regulatory law protects consumers with the statement that "just and reasonable" tariffs have to be charged, imprudent expenditures are inconsistent with that law, and no further notice is then required under applicable law. This statement is quite powerful when considering the legal status of regulatory methodology. Chapter 7 revisits it in examining the need to legitimize the regulatory methodology.

Figure 5.1. Average tariff determination process

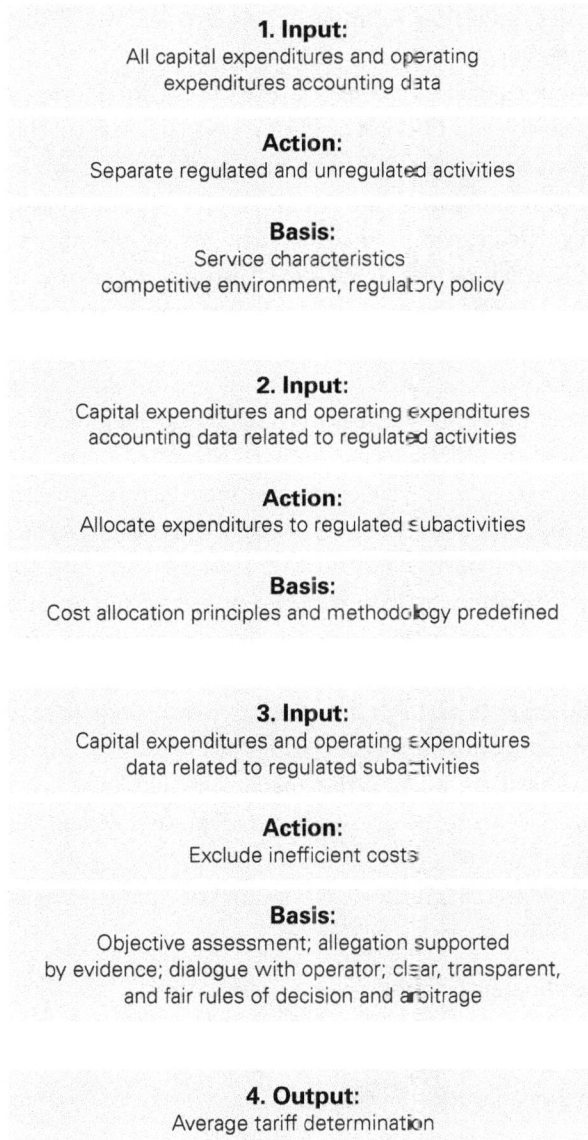

1. Input:
All capital expenditures and operating
expenditures accounting data

Action:
Separate regulated and unregulated activities

Basis:
Service characteristics
competitive environment, regulatory policy

2. Input:
Capital expenditures and operating expenditures
accounting data related to regulated activities

Action:
Allocate expenditures to regulated subactivities

Basis:
Cost allocation principles and methodology predefined

3. Input:
Capital expenditures and operating expenditures
data related to regulated subactivities

Action:
Exclude inefficient costs

Basis:
Objective assessment; allegation supported
by evidence; dialogue with operator; clear, transparent,
and fair rules of decision and arbitrage

4. Output:
Average tariff determination

Source: Authors.

5

Full exclusion of cost items

This section examines the possible full exclusion of some costs incurred for regulated activities. All costs related to unregulated activities should already have been excluded, as detailed in chapter 3.[12]

From an economic perspective, only expenses useful for delivering the regulated service should be recovered through tariff charges to the users of the regulated service. Typically, regulators might exclude ex ante lines of costs such as sponsorships, lobbying expenses, donations, or some advertising costs not considered useful for delivering the regulated service.[13] In a 2000 price review of electricity distribution, the Office of the Regulator-General, Victoria, Australia, excluded all advertising and marketing costs related to campaigns that do not specifically include customers' information or incentives to use energy more efficiently.

A more sensitive issue relates to *management fees* or *related-party transactions*. The regulated operator pays these fees to companies belonging to the same group for specific services (legal, financial, technical, marketing). The rationale for the provision of these services is that operators often belong to large international groups. They consider it more efficient to purchase specific services (services requiring expertise that cannot be found within the operator's company) from the mother company or another company within the group than from an outside company. Because of the size of these management fees (in some cases as high as 3 percent of revenue), some regulators argue that they should be assimilated to return on capital or should be limited in time. Regarding the latter treatment, the argument is that the operator should organize a proper transfer of knowledge to the local regulated operator. This means that, in time, the operator should lower its reliance on the mother company's expertise, progressively reducing payments to the mother company. The regulatory position varies from country to country and even from sector to sector. Chapter 6 presents more detail on this cost item and related issues. As a general rule, regulators should

- have a clear and public position on management fees,
- review in detail the nature of the services performed under management fee arrangements, and
- assess the rationale for these arrangements in view of the characteristics of the local company and its environment.

Marginal and incremental costs are not historical costs. Rather, they are estimates of the future cost of the service. Therefore, estimating them involves estimating future demand for the good or service in question, future capital costs of production facilities, future costs of raw materials and energy, and so on. In that sense, their estimation can be complex.

Partial exclusion of incurred expenses

The partial exclusion of incurred expenses relates to the delicate issue of "excessive" expenses. In a competitive environment a company operating under inefficient management would produce or deliver goods or services at a cost that would put it out of business very quickly because of the presence of competitors operating more efficiently. The objective of regulation is to simulate the positive effects of a competitive environment, so that the benefits of efficiency can be passed on to users through lower tariffs. This objective is enforced through the level of costs that will be allowed by the regulator for tariff determination. The regulator excludes all excessive costs such as excessive capital expenditures, excessive salaries, excessive costs of energy or water purchases, and so on.

Excessive expenses result from poor management. More specifically, they arise from

- "gold-plating" behavior, or investing in the most expensive equipment or producing the most expensive service regardless of the need or efficiency of the operation to maximize returns without diminishing sales;
- lack of good technical analysis; or
- lack of appropriate organizational procedures.

The issue of excessive costs is complex. Consider the case of excessive costs of energy or water purchases by a distribution company in the utilities sector. Excessive costs can arise through failure to optimize purchasing contracts or through use of expensive energy without consideration for cheaper alternatives. These problems can occur because of bad management or because of poorly designed cost pass-through mechanisms or indexation formulas that can undercut the incentive for replacing some costly energy sources with lower-cost alternatives.[14]

In many countries, however, the price of energy and other inputs bought by a distribution company could be excessive not because of a nonoptimized contract or failure to consider alternative sources, but because of the lack of competition upstream. A regulator who compares prices with those in other regions or countries and excludes a percentage of incurred expenses on that basis could be making the wrong decision. The excessive price is exogenous to a cost-minimizing regulated firm. In this situation, the regulator might need help from other agencies (for instance, competition agencies) before deciding whether a cost is imprudent.

The principles, process, and methodology that the regulator uses to decide to exclude some inefficient costs should be clearly established and made public before the license to operate the regulated company is awarded. The regulator cannot exclude inefficient costs as a discretionary exercise.

A few criteria and guidelines

Regulators should take into account several criteria and guidelines when assessing an operator's data to verify compliance with the operator's obligations and operation under efficient management.

Presumption of prudent management

The regulator's work should not interfere with day-to-day management of the firm. For example, the regular review of capital expenditures should not lead to constant second-guessing of management decisions. The regulator should avoid overregulation and micromanagement, which create excessive risks and uncertainty that can deter investment. It should always express its doubts on the basis of rational and quantified information. In the United States there is a legal presumption in favor of utility management.[15] The burden of proof lies with the regulator or the party challenging management decisions. In countries with no explicit legal texts or jurisprudence, this issue is a sensitive one, especially given the problem of asymmetric information and the absence of proper release of information. How can the burden of proof lie with a party (the regulator) that lacks access to detailed information regarding the decision it challenges?

Realism

The financial situation of the operator should be taken into account. Even if motivated, disallowance of costs might be limited to maintaining the operator's solvency and investment capacity, thereby avoiding the greater damage to ratepayers that would result from the operator's insolvency and bankruptcy. The regulator should ensure that the operator implements appropriate management systems and controls to avoid imprudent costs in the future.

Materiality

Regulators have to restrict their analysis to significant amounts that affect tariffs, because they have limited capacity for intervention and analysis.

Objective assessment: Findings of mismanagement

Regulators should base their conclusions on objective and quantitative analysis. Avoidable costs should be estimated on a rational basis. An allegation of management imprudence should be supported by evidence.

Assessment of management decisions should always be performed on the basis of the specific context in which the decisions were taken: under the same circumstances, would reasonable managers have incurred the same expenses?

Regulators should use a comparative and benchmarking approach to make their point. They could look at medians of other local comparative businesses or, if such data are not available, at comparable businesses in the region. They should compare cost percentages, tariffs, and similar data, always taking into account local and regional differences (initial state of assets, specific geographical conditions, and the like).

Regulators can use historical information for evidence of abnormal expenses by comparing cost budgets with real expenses and asking for explanations of differences (overbudgets).

The detailed organizational flowchart of the company is a good source of information. It can help regulators understand the chain of control for expenses and check that proper management control and processes are in place (methodologies in project management, construction, quality assurance, and quality control).

In measuring efficiency, regulators can compare operators' performances in many ways. The main methods are

- *price-based index numbers* for measuring productivity as a ratio of output and input price index;
- *stochastic frontier analysis*, an econometric method that estimates a production or cost frontier; and
- *data envelopment analysis*, a linear programming method that constructs a nonparametric production frontier.[16]

5.7. Regulatory accounting and auditing of regulated companies

Regulatory accounting often requires assurances that information provided by regulated companies is accurate. Requests for such assurances should be proportionate to the problem to be addressed and the resources involved. If the regulator plans to rely heavily on the reported information, some verification of the data may be required. The regulator is unlikely to have the resources or the access to the data systems for this verification.

Specifying auditing requirements involves decisions about

- auditor eligibility,
- the process for appointing the auditor,
- the auditor's duty of care,
- the audit standard,
- the pro forma of the audit report, and
- the consequences of a qualified audit report.

Eligibility to be the auditor

Because the regulatory audit shares many tasks with the statutory audit, allowing the statutory auditor to be the regulatory auditor may avoid duplication and reduce costs. Often, however, this strategy may conflict with the desire to ensure a higher level of independence. A typical requirement is that the auditor possess recognized audit qualifications; some regulators have added further requirements, such as that the audit team be led by a partner or principal of an audit firm. Despite scepticism borne of recent audit experience, regulators should recognize that risks to professional standards and reputation do discipline auditors.

Process for appointing the auditor

Once the eligibility criteria have been set, the regulator need not be involved in selection of the auditor. In practice, however, regulators have often established requirements for the selection of auditors. For example, approval of the regulator may be required before the auditor is appointed, or the operator may be required to select the auditor from a panel determined by the regulator.

Duty of care of the auditor

In a normal audit, the auditor's duty of care is to the board of directors. This duty reflects the role of the board as representatives of the shareholders and the role of the audit in ensuring that the shareholders' interests are preserved. In contrast, the regulatory audit serves a different function, and regulatory accounts routinely specify that the auditor owes a duty of care to both the operator's board and the regulator, or that the primary duty of care is to the regulator. A joint accountability may be formalized through a tripartite agreement of the auditor, the operator, and the regulator.

Audit standard

Various levels of assurance can be provided (see figure 5.2). The highest level of assurance is provided by a normal audit; this level of assurance is the one specified in most cases. But a lower level of assurance can be specified when it provides a more appropriate balance between the costs of the process and the needs of the regulator.

In a normal business audit, a matter is material if it is likely to prejudice the understanding of an entity's financial position—that is, when the matter is not consistent with a "true and fair view" of the entity as a whole. The regulator has a somewhat different concern and requires assurance that the regulatory accounts present a true and fair view of the *regulated component* of the entity or of the related parties. This concern has led to modification of the standard of materiality. Whether the regulated activity is the major activity of the entity is an immaterial matter, because the regulated activity may have a material effect on reporting of the unregulated activities. For this reason, some regulators have established additional

Figure 5.2. International Federation of Accountants framework for auditing and related services

	Auditing	——— Related services ———		
Nature of service	Audit	Review	Agreed-on procedures	Compilation
Comparative level of assurance provided by the auditor	High, but not absolute, assurance	Moderate assurance	No assurance	No assurance
Report provided	Positive assurance on assertion(s)	Negative assurance on assertion(s)	Factual findings of procedures	Identification of information compiled

Source: www.pwcglobal.com.

requirements. The Queensland Competition Authority, for example, specifies that a matter is material if it results in an inappropriate allocation of costs between regulated activities and unregulated activities.

Pro forma of the audit report

Regulators have commonly provided pro formas (templates) of the audit report and directors' responsibility statement. The pro forma reports have been modeled on standard corporate pro forma reports and adjusted for any differences in the level of audit and materiality tests.

Consequence of a qualified audit report

The audit requirements should specify the steps to be followed in the event of a qualified audit report. No formal response is needed. The regulator may simply accept the qualified audit. More likely, it will specify some capacity, including (in ascending order) capacity to

- request further changes,
- direct the nature of the changes to be made, and
- appoint a new auditor or request the utility to engage a new auditor.

Additional reading and resources

Arizu, Beatriz, Luiz Maurer, and Bernard Tenenbaum. 2004. "Pass Through of Power Purchase Costs: Regulatory Challenges and International Practices." Energy and Mining Sector Board Discussion Paper 10, Energy and Mining Sector Board, World Bank, Washington, DC.

Estache, A., and P. Burns. 1998. "Information, Accounting, and Regulation of Concessioned Infrastructure Monopolies." Policy Research Working Paper 2034, World Bank, Washington, DC.

Goodman, L.S. 1998. *The Process of Ratemaking*. Vienna, VA: Public Utilities Reports, Inc.

Green, R. J., and M. Rodriguez Pardina. 1999. *Resetting Price Controls for Privatized Utilities: A Manual for Regulators*. Washington, DC: Economic Development Institute of the World Bank.

Ofgem (Office of Gas and Electricity Markets). 2001. "The Role of Regulatory Accounts in Regulated Industries." London.

Notes

1. For more detail on this fundamental issue, refer to annex 2 on regulatory modeling and to the World Bank Institute's CD-ROM "Financial Modeling of Regulatory Policy: Introduction to Theory and Practice" (World Bank 2002).

2. Regulators also use the information to define quality standards, assess the financial health of the company, evaluate the relative efficiency of the company, and so on.

3. Prices must be set at an affordable level. Users' capacity to pay is an important factor to consider in regulatory policy.

4. This behavior could take the form, for example, of subsidizing international calls by national calls.

5. For accuracy and clarity, regulators usually provide electronic spreadsheets with preformatted tables to be filled in (see chapter 6).

6. For a list of indicators, see annex 5.

7. See chapter 7 for details on information exchange mechanisms.

8. Such data are needed unless the regulator uses either a rate of return on the rate-base approach, an historic test year, or a high-powered incentive approach that fully unlinks the regulated price path from the actual costs of the utility.

9. Statutory accounts have to comply in full with all accounting standards.

10. See Estache, Wodon, and Foster (2002) for practical guidelines and methods to help policy makers, reformers, and regulators develop diagnoses and strategies to meet policy objectives.

11. In the United States the concept of honest, economic, and efficient management is used in regulatory decisions. The phrase "honest, economic, and efficient management" made its initial appearance in a rule of ratemaking of the Emergency Railroad Transportation Act of 1933.

12. If, in some cases, regulators allow *costs distortions* (cross-subsidies) for specific political, social, and economic reasons, they should precisely quantify and preapprove the distortions as well as make them fully transparent.

13. Of course, the company can incur these expenses. They simply will not be taken into account in tariff determination.

14. Arizu, Maurer, and Tenenbaum (2004) discuss the options for passing through energy purchase costs when wholesale markets are competitive but retail prices remain controlled, highlighting the difficulties.

15. Several court decisions specify this presumption. For more detail, see Goodman 1998, 860.

16. Explaining these methods goes beyond the scope of this volume. Interested readers should refer to Coelli and others (2003).

Chapter 6

Core Issues in Regulatory Accounting

This chapter further develops the core issues in regulatory accounting:

- *separation of activities,*
- *regulatory asset base determination (concept and valuation and depreciation),*
- *depreciation policies of the regulatory asset base, and*
- *related-party transactions and transfer pricing.*

Separation of the activities of regulated operators into regulated activities and unregulated activities is the core motivation of regulatory accounting. Such separation is essential for facilitating control of regulatory objectives. This chapter shows how each regulatory alternative—single till regulation, separation of companies, and accounting separation of activities within a company—has different implications for information requirements. The chapter also shows how the concepts of cost accounting and cost classification introduced in chapter 4 are used in regulatory accounting.

Valuation of the regulatory asset base and specification of depreciation profiles are also critical tasks of the regulator. Definition of the regulatory asset base is related to the regulatory perimeter, a concept introduced in chapter 5. This chapter explains how the valuation and depreciation options of the regulatory asset base are at the core of tariff determination, and how regulatory options could diverge from what is implemented in standard statutory accounts.

Chapter 5 examined the issue of management fees. This chapter reviews the more general context of related-party transactions and transfer pricing, which regulators need to identify clearly. These topics are central to regulatory objectives, and they present particularities that call for accounting treatments that differ substantially from management and statutory accounting treatments.

For most topics, regulators can choose from a wide range of alternatives, depending on the characteristics of the sector, the legal framework, and the weight given to various regulatory objectives, among other factors. These alternatives are to a large extent interdependent. Therefore, the need for consistency among the options chosen for each topic is great.

Consistency must be maintained over time as well. Adherence to the same criteria from year to year helps to reduce uncertainty and perceived risk among investors.

6.1. Separation of activities

As a result of technology change in many infrastructure sectors and restructuring to introduce competition, regulated activities and unregulated activities coexist in most companies. The regulatory treatment applied in this situation is particularly important.

Treatment of unregulated activities should be framed to meet general regulatory objectives, particularly preserving incentives for productive efficiency, avoiding distortions in competitive markets, and ensuring that users benefit from efficiency gains. Before analyzing the alternatives for addressing unregulated activities, regulators will need to identify different types of activities and situations to develop a more complete framework for their analysis. Different criteria may be used for this analysis:

- Unregulated activities could be separated according to whether or not they use assets of the regulated service.
- Unregulated activities could be separated according to whether their markets are competitive or separately regulated monopolistic activities.
- Activities could be separated on the basis of the degree of vertical integration of the unregulated activity with the regulated activity and the extent to which that integration is part of the industry's value chain.

The first distinction, between unregulated activities that use the assets of the regulated service and those that do not, is crucial to the productive efficiency objective. In general, the performance of unregulated activities using assets of the regulated activity assumes the existence of some degree of economies of scope. A typical example is an electricity distribution company's use of the electric company's poles to lay down television cables. Using the poles as a common asset is more efficient than employing two separate sets of poles.

Economies of scope imply that the joint production cost of regulated activities and unregulated activities is lower than the sum of the costs of both activities performed separately. When this is the case, development of the unregulated activity by the regulated operator increases efficiency; hence, a net welfare loss would result if the regulated operator were banned from carrying out the unregulated activity. The problem is to clearly determine how greater efficiency in the use of assets will be shared by the operator and the users (who pay for it in the long run through regulated service tariffs).

Now consider the second distinction, wherein unregulated activities are separated according to whether their markets are competitive. If the unregulated activity develops in a competitive market, the operator has strong incentives to distort the allocation of costs, increasing them for the regulated activity and reducing them for the activity in the competitive market. In this way, the operator recovers costs through the regulated tariffs and improves its position in the competitive market, obtaining extraordinary gains. An electricity transmission company using its system to lay down fiber-optic cables and enter the telecommunications business is an example of a regulated utility entering a competitive market. This move not only affects the regulated activity, but may also distort the competitive market, because a bad allocation of common costs might bestow an unfair competitive advantage on a service provider that can recover part of its costs in a captive market.[1] If the regulated activity is carried out in another regulated market, no such incentive exists.

Finally, consider the third distinction: the degree to which the unregulated activity is vertically integrated with the regulated activity. If the unregulated activity is vertically integrated with the regulated activity, the firm has greater incentives to influence the unregulated market by manipulating the regulated activity. An airport operator's ownership of substantial interest in an airline is an example of vertical integration of a regulated activity into a competitive sector.

Such integration gives rise to the regulatory access problem: what to do when a regulated company is to provide a service—access—to its competitors in an unregulated market. The tariff criteria for the essential facility (the one competitors need as an input to provide the service) are crucial to avoid distortions in the competitive market and to achieve the regulatory objectives of sustainability and allocative efficiency.

When both activities are not part of the same value chain, as in the electricity and telecommunications example, the problem is less serious, because competitors are not also customers of the regulated operator. However, the incentives of the regulated operator to allocate more costs to the regulated activity in order to improve its competitiveness in the unregulated market remain.

Regulatory alternatives

This section deals with the alternatives that can be used with regulated operators in treating unregulated activities. It covers the alternatives' advantages and disadvantages in terms of the regulatory objectives mentioned above.

Single till regulation

Single till regulation assumes that all revenue from unregulated activities is considered on the revenue account of the regulated activity. In many cases, because of inadequate information, the costs of the unregulated activity are assumed to equal its revenue, and that consequently separating unregulated activities for regulatory purposes is unnecessary.

This approach was proposed for regulating airports in the United Kingdom. All revenue arising from unregulated activities within the airport, such as shops and restaurants, would be taken into account in estimating the revenue requirements of the regulated activity.

The main advantage of this approach is its simplicity. Only information on the total revenue and costs of all activities is required. Separation of regulated activities and unregulated activities is unnecessary.

The drawbacks of this approach, though, clearly exceed the advantage of simplicity. First, the approach clearly goes against the objective of productive efficiency, because it takes away any incentive for the operator to develop unregulated activities under the concession. As long as all of the additional revenue from unregulated activities results in a reduction of regulated revenue, the company has no incentive to generate revenue.

Second, this alternative results in extremely unattractive incentives for allocative efficiency. In the airport example, the revenue from unregulated activities increases with the degree of congestion of terminals, driving down the regulated tariffs for the terminals' use. This phenomenon sends the wrong signals for efficient allocation of resources.

Separation of companies

An alternative is to require that regulated activities and unregulated activities be developed by different legal entities. This separation can take two forms.

The less strict form of separation requires that the unregulated activities are performed by a separate legal entity but does not prohibit common ownership. Thus a regulated operator or its shareholders can own a subsidiary company performing unregulated activities.

The stricter form of separation imposes restrictions on cross-ownership of regulated activities and unregulated activities. The regulated company, and in some cases even its shareholders, cannot own companies that render services or sell products in unregulated activities. Under this stricter form of the approach, the problem of unregulated activities disappears for the regulator—but at the cost of preventing the company and its shareholders (and indirectly its customers) from taking advantage of potential economies of scope between activities. In summary, the regulatory load is minimized at the expense of the company's productive efficiency.

Separation of activities and accounting

The two alternatives discussed above are extreme cases that either ignore or prohibit unregulated activities within the regulated company. In general, these alternatives are not efficient, and most countries decide instead to demand separate accounting of regulated activities and unregulated activities. This separate information becomes the basic input for regulatory allocation and determination of the operator's revenue requirement. This input can be supported by "behavioral requirements," such as limits on sharing of information between regulated entities and nonregulated entities and provision of information to customers. Box 6.1 provides an example of an approach that combines various *ring-fencing requirements*.

The next section deals with some of the key elements needed to create a basic framework of information for regulatory accounting and the regulatory alternatives for use of that information.

Accounting separation of activities

Accounting separation of regulated activities and unregulated activities appears to be the most common alternative used by regulators to treat unregulated activities. This alternative requires a cost accounting system, as defined in chapter 3, but one adapted to the regulator's needs, as explained in chapters 4 and 5. The regulator will need to specify segmentation of activities (functions) and to specify classification and segmentation of costs (to assess the efficiency level of particular lines of costs).

Using the concepts of cost classifications presented in chapter 3, costs could be separated, from a regulatory point of view, in several ways. They could be

- divided into operation costs and maintenance costs,
- categorized by function (for example, in the case of a vertically integrated electricity company, by generation, transmission, distribution, and supply),

Box 6.1. Treatment of unregulated activities in New South Wales, Australia

The Australian National Electricity Code requires regional regulators to develop guidelines for *ring fencing* (separating regulated activities from unregulated activities). The Independent Pricing and Regulatory Tribunal (IPART) has developed various proposals for these guidelines, as have other regional and national regulatory authorities, such as the Australian Competition and Consumer Commission.

IPART defines ring fencing as "the clear separation of subsidiaries or divisions of a company that may be viewed as having competitive advantages in their dealings with each other." IPART believes that such separation will help the regulator identify the true nature and provision costs of the activities that need to be regulated (because they constitute natural monopolies).

Some of the guidelines suggested by IPART are the following:

- Legally separate the entity through which a network service provider provides network services from any other entity through which it conducts business.
- Establish and maintain consolidated and separate accounts for prescribed services and other services provided by (1) the transmission network service provider and (2) the distribution network service provider.
- Allocate costs between prescribed services and other services provided by the transmission network service provider and between prescribed distribution services and other services provided by the distribution network service provider.
- Limit the flow of information between the network service provider and any other person.
- Where the potential for a competitive disadvantage exists, limit the flow of information between the parts of the network service provider's business that provide prescribed services and the parts of the network that provide any other services, and between the parts of the network service provider's business that provide prescribed distribution services and the parts that provide any other services.

Source: Authors.

- divided into controllable costs and uncontrollable costs (some regulatory schemes focus incentives on controllable costs and adopt pass-through mechanisms for uncontrollable costs), or
- divided into central costs (for example, head office) costs and functional costs.

Regulators usually require clear identification of other specific lines of costs, such as regulatory fees (fees paid to the regulatory authority), concession fees (if any), and management fees (all related-party transactions above a certain amount).

Energy purchases are of specific interest to the regulator, particularly when cost pass-through mechanisms or inappropriately designed indexation formulas undercut incentives to replace costly energy sources with lower-cost alternatives.

Table 6.1 presents an example of the classification of an electricity operator's operating costs. These costs are divided into functional costs and central costs. Items in boldface represent typical uncontrollable costs that should be aggregated to allow an analysis of controllable costs and uncontrollable costs as well as an analysis of total operating costs.

This example assumes that the company is involved in two regulated activities (electricity transmission and distribution) and two unregulated activities (electricity generation and trading). The first separation requires identification of the direct (or functional) costs of each phase. In general, these costs are relatively easy to identify, because they are directly incurred in development of the activity. With respect

Table 6.1. Classification of costs for an electricity operator

	Unregulated activities		Regulated activities		
	Generation	Trading	Transmission	Distribution	Total
Functional costs					
Personnel					
Goods and materials					
Contracted services					
Lubricants					
Fuels					
Total functional costs					
Central costs					
Management					
Trading					

Source: Authors.

to these direct costs, regulators will require details on cost nature, such as personnel, intermediary products, third-party services, and so on.

For regulated activities, a second level of disaggregation will allow for more detailed analysis of subactivities. Table 6.2 shows a possible classification of subactivities in electricity production.

Chapter 4 noted that the electricity regulator in Argentina decided to apply the activity-based costing approach to give users additional information about the use of all the resources directly or indirectly associated with each of the activities developed by the distribution companies, because the services provided by these companies should be affected by a share of resource costs. The accounts selected by this regulator are classified according to activities, which are further classified by type of good and nature of the associated cost, as shown in table 6.3.

This strategy facilitates control of the use of resources by relating them to activities. Separation of subactivities is unnecessary for unregulated activities. The regulator needs only to identify the costs shared by the regulated activities and the unregulated activities. When the regulated activity purchases a service from its unregulated arm, the regulator will need to ensure that the price is reasonable and that the action is not an attempt to shift costs and profits between the two activities. (These cases are discussed in the section below on related-party transactions.)

Some regulators require that when the costs of third-party contracted services exceed a certain threshold they be broken down by cost nature as if the activities were provided in-house. For example, the Office of Water Service ([Ofwat] the UK water regulator) sets the threshold at 20 percent of the activity costs, but it encourages firms to break down the costs of contracted activities well below that limit.

Depending on the structure of the operator and the nature of its market, the regulator may establish criteria for disaggregating costs according to location, technical system, technology, and other dimensions. For example, if the operator serves an important geographic area with a high degree of heterogeneity (in terms of customer density and demand composition, for example), the regulator may require the operator to identify the cost of serving each area. If the operator provides services in more than one system, as in the case of water companies providing services in separate cities or villages that are not interconnected, the regulator needs information on the revenues and costs arising from each system even when it decides to apply homogeneous tariffs across all systems. The reason is that separation of revenues and costs allows identification of potential flows of funding or cross-subsidies among the systems.

Table 6.2. Subactivities in regulated and unregulated activities of an electricity operator

Phase	Subphase	Function	Investment
Generation		To turn primary energy into electricity	Power stations (hydroelectric, thermal, gas powered, coal powered, nuclear, wind, solar); capacity from 1–1,000 megawatts
Transformation		To turn electricity generation voltage level into transmission voltage level; to allow long-distance transmission of large capacities	Transformers, bars, protection, metering and control equipment, and civil works
Transmission		To transport electricity from generation sites to the boundaries of large consumption centers; usually mesh system	Networks of 115–765 kilovolts, with capacity of 50–2,000 megawatts
Distribution	Transformation	To turn very high voltage electricity into lower voltage to facilitate transmission in a certain geographical area	Transformers, bars, protection, metering and control equipment, and civil works
	Subtransmission	To distribute the electricity received from very high-voltage/high-voltage transformer stations to high-voltage/medium-voltage transformer stations for regional distribution	Networks of 66–220 kilovolts, with capacity of 35–200 megavolt amperes
	Transformation	To receive electricity from subtransmission systems and turn it into lower voltage to allow local distribution, usually more than one distribution level	Transformers, bars, protection, metering and control equipment, and civil works
	Transformation posts	To receive electricity from feeders and distributors and convert it to the primary voltage level of direct users	Transformer (three phase, two phase, and single phase), civil works (air, land, underground), and protection equipment; capacity of 3–1,000 kilovolt amperes
	Secondary distribution in low voltage	To distribute energy from medium-voltage/low-voltage transformation posts to users; always radial from the standpoint of operation; from the standpoint of construction, usually sections between circuit ends for reconfiguration	Networks made by conventional overhead lines, preassembled, and underground wires; voltage levels of 110–400 volts
	Invoicing	Meter reading and invoices to customers	Installation and maintenance of meters and invoicing and collection systems
Trading		Purchase and sale of electricity by contract or in the spot market; potentially competitive activity	

Source: Authors.

6

Table 6.3. Example of activity classification by electricity regulator

Level 1: Chapters	Level 2: Items	Level 3: Activities and subactivities	Levels 4–5: Type of goods	Level 6: Nature of cost
7. Expenditures	3. Technical operation	40. Transformation— preventive maintenance	1. Substations– 1.1. Substations high voltage/ high voltage	1. Payroll 2. Materials 3. Contracted services and others

Source: Authors.

6.2. Regulatory asset base determination

From an economic perspective, tariff determination should meet several regulatory objectives, including sustainability, allocative efficiency, productive efficiency, and equity. Economic and financial sustainability require that tariffs generate enough revenue to cover the economic cost of service provision, including a return on capital. The rate of return must be determined on the basis of the opportunity cost of capital—what could be earned from the best alternative investment with similar risk. However, this approach covers only one part of the problem. The regulator must also determine the composition and value of the regulatory asset base to which this rate of return would apply.

This key part of the regulatory process raises two related problems. First, the regulator must determine which investments by the regulated operator are specific to the service and also meet efficiency and prudence criteria. Second, the regulator must decide how to value these investments for regulatory purposes. In the context of regulatory accounting, the relation between the regulatory asset base and the book value of the operator's assets is important to consider, as is the matter of how to reconcile the two if they do not match.

Asset base valuation

Regardless of the approach selected to quantify the asset base, certain general principles apply, such as that the asset base should reflect mainly the value of the assets engaged in the public service. In most cases the approach focuses on the entries under the assets account in the balance sheet, updated as necessary, for example, for depreciation (Goodman 1998, 732). Discussion of the most appropriate way to value the asset base is not new. At the end of the nineteenth century, in *Smyth vs. Ames*, the U.S. Supreme Court ruled that

> the basis of all calculations as to the reasonableness of rates to be charged by a cor-
> poration maintaining a highway under legislative sanction must be the fair value
> of the property being used by it for the convenience of the public. And in order to
> ascertain that value, the original cost of construction, the amount expended in per-
> manent improvements, the amount and market value of its bonds and stocks, the
> present as compared with the original cost of construction, the probable earning
> capacity of the property under particular rates prescribed by statute, and the sum
> required to meet operating expenses, are all matters for consideration, and are to be
> given such weight as may be just and right in each case. We do not say that there
> may not be other matters to be regarded in estimating the value of the property.
> What the company is entitled to ask is a fair return upon the value of that which it
> employs for the public convenience. On the other hand, what the public is entitled
> to demand is that no more be exacted from it for the use of a public highway than
> the services rendered by it are reasonably worth (Goodman 1998, 755).

Three approaches for asset base determination can be identified in this court decision:

- *historic value* (original building cost),
- *market value* (amount and market value of the firm's bonds and stocks), and
- *replacement value* (current building cost).

The following sections briefly examine the advantages and disadvantages of these methods, which remain the most frequently discussed in the literature and applied in regulatory practice at the international level.

Historical cost

Traditionally, companies have recorded the value of their fixed assets on a historical cost basis, which continues to be the basis applied in most statutory accounts (see chapter 3). The use of a historical cost basis is consistent with the role of statutory accounts in allowing investors to review the quality of stewardship of their invest-ments by management. Investors are interested in the return earned on their actual investment rather than on some notional asset base.

Market value

When a stock is listed, the market value provides the best guide to expectations of future revenues derived from the company's assets—and therefore the company's economic worth. In a regulated environment, however, this market value introduces a circularity problem, whereby future revenues depend on prices that in turn depend on the asset base derived from future revenues.

When companies are not listed on a public stock exchange, regulators must use estimates of the discounted cash flows arising from that asset in the future. Again, the circularity problem limits the usefulness of this methodology for regulatory purposes.

Replacement cost

An alternative form of valuation is to consider the cost of building the infrastructure at current prices, but even a replacement cost measure is not a true reflection of the economic worth of the assets. It fails to take into account technological change and thus to capture the extent to which more efficient modern assets can substitute for existing assets. It also assumes that the existing asset configuration is the most efficient configuration.

Two refinements of the replacement cost methodology seek to address these issues. The first is revaluation of assets on the basis of modern equivalent asset values—for example, by substituting a gas-fired power plant for an equivalent size coal-fired plant. The second refinement is creation of depreciated optimized replacement cost estimates. This refinement extends the first refinement by modeling the optimal asset configuration to deliver the service at the current time. For example, one large plant might replace two smaller generation plants under such a valuation.

When multiple values are possible (for example, when the depreciated optimized replacement cost differs from the market value), the appropriate rule to apply from an efficiency point of view is the *deprival rule,* which states that the value of the assets to their owner is lower than their replacement cost (however defined) and higher than their market value or scrap value. Essentially, this value represents the value that an investor could obtain for the assets and therefore the value at which the investor should be compensated for being deprived of these assets.

Formally, the deprival rule can be expressed as follows:

$$\text{Value} = Min[DORC, Max\{PV, SV\}],$$

where *DORC* is depreciated optimal replacement cost valuation of the asset (replacement cost), *PV* is present value of cash flows earned from the asset (market value), and *SV* is scrap value of the asset.

Regulatory asset base composition

In dealing with the asset base composition, the regulator must consider principles that may not arise in asset base valuation in unregulated companies.

Assets

In regulated companies, the rate base reflects primarily the assets in public service rather than a quantity of stocks or bonds devoted to the public service. The focus is on properties on the asset side of the balance sheet adjusted only as needed by reference to various reserves on the liability side.

In deciding whether particular assets should be included in the rate base calculation, regulators may apply the principle that only assets in service in the test year or the near-term period should be included. Whatever the method of rate base valuation, investors are entitled to a return only on that portion of their investment that is used and useful in the public service, assuming a reasonable planning period.[2]

Intangible property is rarely includible in the rate base.[3] For example, the Massachusetts Regulatory Commission held that intangible costs that benefit ratepayers over more than one year are appropriately capitalized and included in the rate base. Such costs would include, for example, computer software and organization costs related to mergers involving the regulated company.

Goodwill

Goodwill can be described as a global concept that captures a set of company activities related to superior earning power, such as customer loyalty, employees' expertise, management capabilities, and all the other intangible factors that motivate people to do business with the company.

The U.S. Federal Communication Commission noted that traditionally such excess acquisitions costs are partly or wholly excluded from rate bases, because these costs typically benefit the seller, not the ratepayer, and do not contribute to the plant supporting the regulated service. In arguing for inclusion of goodwill in the rate base, the regulated operator bears the burden of showing that its costs result from arms-length bargaining and that the net efficiency gains result in concrete, tangible benefits to ratepayers.

Whether the costs of obtaining a franchise, as distinguished from the value of the franchise itself, should be included in the rate base is debatable. Regulatory commissions uniformly reject capitalized values of company franchises. When government confers the right to operate a utility, the only capitalizable assets are the land, equipment, and buildings for which capital outlays have been made, even though a market for the franchise may exist.

Deferred operating costs and regulatory assets

When the operator, with the regulator's approval, postpones the collection of a cost from ratepayers, it may be allowed to create a deferred cost or a regulatory asset on its books for a stated period. It thereby capitalizes the cost and will thereafter amortize the cost through charges to ratepayers, with or without inclusion of the unamortized balance in the rate base. Deferred costs are included in the rate base only when ratepayers have not yet been called on to bear the costs in any of the rates. If ratepayers have already paid the deferred cost, that cost may not be included in the rate base. A utility typically uses deferred costs and regulatory assets to account for the period between the in-service date of a major generating plant and the time that its costs can be reflected in new rates.

Leased property

Regulators generally distinguish between a *capital lease* and an *operating lease.* Only the properties under a long-term capital lease qualify for inclusion in the capital structure and rate base. Such inclusion does not automatically follow for every capital lease. Lease payments under operating leases are included in operating expenses on the operator's income statement and taken as an allowable expense for ratemaking purposes.

Third-party contributions

Most agencies will deduct from the rate base any part of the capital that either has been donated (or deposited) and bears no capital cost to the company, or is otherwise maintained on the company's books at no cost to investors. The widely followed rule is that the property account shall include no cost or value for facilities or land contributed or paid for by government agencies, individuals, or others. Alternatively, such sums can be carried as booked investment—but,at a zero cost of capital or deducted from the allowance for working capital and hence from the rate base.

Working capital

The regulatory asset base includes not only physical assets but also liquid funds needed for the operation of the business. These funds are known as *working capital* and are based on the funds that the operator must keep on hand to continue day-to-day operations. The working capital allowance takes into account short-term assets and liabilities. It assumes that a well-managed company will have a reasonable margin of current assets over current liabilities (that is, net working capital) on hand at all times. Typically, working capital requirements are assessed through a lead/lag study that analyses the time between the utility's provision of a service and receipt of revenues (the "lag") and the time between the utility's receipt of goods or services and payment for those goods or services (the "lead"). The resulting working capital requirements are then included in the rate base on which the operator will be given the opportunity to earn a fair return.

Other principles

In dealing with the asset base composition, the regulator must also consider the following principles:

- The rate base is usually a net valuation figure after deduction of the current depreciation reserve, including all past accumulated depreciation on the same assets. The depreciation reserve must be deducted from the rate base, because a depreciation charge is a financial transaction between consumers and the operator. Because consumers contribute revenue for the investment amortization, the recovered depreciation should be deducted from the property valuation. Otherwise, consumers pay returns on property values that are already amortized.
- Losses on the sale of property or on purchases made by the operator that it recognized by a reduction in retained earnings are not properly included in the rate base.
- A regulated company cannot properly attempt to recover prior operating losses through inclusion of such losses in the rate base.
- An electric utility is entitled to include a reasonable allowance for coal, oil, and diesel fuel inventories in the rate base.
- In recent years a major issue has been whether deferred taxes on utility books should be included or excluded from the rate base. Most utility regulators exclude those sums, finding that they have been contributed by ratepayers rather than by investors in the regulated company and so carry no associated cost of capital. Alternatively, a treatment equal or equivalent to removal from the rate base would be treatment of deferred taxes as zero cost capital in the rate of return and capital structure computations.
- Regulatory treatment of the differences between forecast and actual capital expenditures depends directly on the regulatory regime adopted, but some cases are worth mentioning. For example, in the United Kingdom capital expenditures larger or smaller than forecast receive asymmetric treatment. If the operator invests more than the capital expenditure approved in the five-year tariff review, the amount over the approved expenditure is not included in the asset base. Thus, the regulator prevents users of the regulated service from paying for excessive capital expenditure—which might be caused by the operator's lack of efficiency. If the capital expenditure is lower than forecast, the regulator allows

the forecast value to be incorporated into the asset base to provide incentives to improve efficiency. When companies spend less in delivering the required outputs than the amount determined at periodic reviews, they may keep the benefits of these capital efficiencies for a specific period of time, after which the benefits are passed on to customers.

Box 6.2 describes the approach of one regulator (the UK's Office of Water Services [Ofwat]) to the problem of establishing and rolling forward the regulatory asset base.

6.3. Depreciation policies of the regulatory asset base

Depreciation is an important issue for the regulator, for several reasons:

- Regulated utilities are capital intensive, and depreciation is a major component of the costs.
- The approach to calculating depreciation is considerably flexible, and the choice of the depreciation profile can smooth prices and cash flows and reduce risks for the investor.
- Changes in depreciation profiles can result in windfall gains and losses if not handled carefully.

Annex 4 provides further analysis of the principles for depreciation and the impacts of different depreciation profiles.

Regulatory approaches to depreciation

The regulator needs to consider the full range of regulatory objectives in setting depreciation requirements. Economic objectives are important, but which of the most commonly used approaches most closely approaches economic depreciation remains unclear. Thus, flexibility in the depreciation profiles is considerable, and the choice of these profiles should be guided by such noneconomic objectives as administrative simplicity, certainty, price stability, and intergenerational equity.

The key requirements for the regulator are the following:

- total (accumulated) depreciation over the asset's life equals the difference between the asset's undepreciated value and the residual value;
- any changes to the depreciation profile have a net present value–neutral effect on prices and the income stream (this insight should follow from the point above); and
- the approach is transparent, administratively simple, and consistent with intergenerational equity.

Box 6.2. Regulatory capital values, Office of Water Services, United Kingdom

The following are regulatory accounting guidelines from Ofwat in the United Kingdom:

- The valuation of initial operating assets should disregard the impact of the regulatory regime which would otherwise imply that the value to the business was the recoverable amount. To date, MEA [modern equivalent asset] values have been reflected in the regulatory accounts with no reference to or inclusion of the value placed on the asset base for regulatory purposes (primarily for price setting). However, over time analysts and investors have increased their focus on the RCV [regulatory capital value], using it as a proxy for market values. Therefore from the 2002–03 financial year onward, the regulatory capital value will be included in a note to the regulatory accounts. This will enable readers of the accounts to assess the value of the assets used for regulatory purposes (the RCV) relative to the largely replacement value of the assets (the MEA value).

- The RCV starts with a direct measure of the value placed on each company's capital and debt by the financial markets following privatisation (or a broadly similar measure for water only companies which were not floated). This is then rolled forward to take account of new capital investment, net of depreciation. The calculation of RCVs is an essential element in Ofwat's price determination process. They also act as a proxy for market values and as such form an important basis for measuring financial performance.

- The Ofwat methodology is effectively a regulatory hybrid to provide equitable treatment between consumers and shareholders. It is based on acquisition costs to ensure that there is no

(continues)

6

Box 6.2. *(continued)*

windfall gain to shareholders. Consumers incur depreciation charges based on current replacement (MEA) costs, so that each period consumers pay for the asset value used in the services supplied.

- The initial RCV is calculated as the average of the market value of each water and sewerage company for the first 200 days for which the shares were listed plus the total value of debt at privatisation. A proxy for the initial market value was used for the water only companies that were not privatised in 1989.

- The value has been adjusted each year to take account of net investment. Capital expenditure to enhance and maintain the network which has been assumed in setting price limits has been added to the value. This is after deducting the amount of depreciation (based on the MEA values of the assets) which has been assumed in setting price limits. Any grants and contributions and associated amortisation are also taken into account. Infrastructure renewals expenditure is not added to the RCV but the movement in the infrastructure renewals accrual or prepayment is included. Adjustments are also made in respect of disposals of land to remove the value of this from the RCV.

- The RCV is adjusted each year by RPI [retail price index] to take account of inflation.

- By setting out clear guidance on RCV methodology and publishing the values of the RCV in the regulatory accounts, transparency will be aided and there will be consistency between the companies. The figures in the reconciliation will be those determined by Ofwat at Periodic Reviews."

Source: Regulatory Accounting Guidelines (RAG) 1.03, Office of Water Services, United Kingdom.

Alternative approaches to depreciation

A range of depreciation methodologies, which vary in complexity and profile of depreciation charges and prices over time, is available to the regulator:

- *Straight-line depreciation:* A constant percentage of the undepreciated asset value is deducted from the opening asset value in each year. This approach is simple and easily applied but may not reflect economic depreciation.
- *Declining balance depreciation:* Depreciation is a constant proportion of the opening asset value. Thus depreciation is front-end loaded (the dollar amount of depreciation is larger in the early years of an asset's life). This approach may better match the economic depreciation of some assets (such as cars) than others (such as buildings).
- *Annuity depreciation:* For a constant annual revenue the net present value of which equals the cost of the asset, the depreciation in each period is the amount left after the deduction of a normal return on the opening value of the asset for the period. This approach, which is similar to repayment of principal on a mortgage, is not often used in business, but it yields a constant price over the asset's life.

Estimation of asset lives

In principle, an asset should be depreciated over its expected productive life. Estimating asset life accurately may be difficult. The condition, even the age, of current assets may not be well known. The long life of infrastructure assets also means that their useful economic life may be difficult to estimate. Some assets (such as water mains or aging gas pipelines) may not be replaced but may instead have their service lives extended through maintenance and renewal technologies. For these assets, a renewal accounting approach may be most appropriate.

There may be circumstances in which the regulator wishes to change the assumed economic life of assets, but the regulator should do so carefully and only when the new assumed life would have a purely prospective impact.

Treatment of depreciation on variations from forecast capital expenditures

As noted in the discussion of the regulatory asset base, actual and forecast capital expenditure will almost certainly vary. Treatment of the difference between the two has important implications for the operator's incentives and should be taken into account in the overall decision about how to roll forward the asset base.[4] One option

6

is to roll forward the asset base between reviews by adding capital expenditure to assets as incurred and depreciating those assets from that point on using the standard depreciation lives. For the operator, this strategy increases incentives to pursue efficiency gains but imposes higher risks.

Alternatively, the asset base could be rolled forward through the addition of actual capital expenditure to the asset base and the deduction of forecast depreciation. This strategy reduces incentives for efficiency improvements, but it also reduces risks from unexpected variations in capital expenditure requirements.

The regulator's primary obligation is to clearly specify the proposed treatment of depreciation in the roll forward of the asset base at the start of the regulatory period and to incorporate this treatment in the accounting rules.

Principles for depreciation

The following principles should guide treatment of depreciation:

- A simple, easily implemented approach to calculating depreciation, such as the use of straight depreciation, is to be preferred.
- Such an approach is unlikely to coincide with economic depreciation, but no single approach is necessarily more likely than another to reflect the economic depreciation of individual assets.
- Applying a uniform approach (but not uniform asset life) to all assets is clearest, simplest, and most easily verified, and it avoids the need to monitor the demarcation between asset classes.
- Maintaining a consistent approach to and assumptions about depreciation over time helps to avoid uncertainty and windfall gains or unexpected losses.
- The option to revise the depreciation profile and assumed asset lives should be left open in light of changing information about asset conditions and lives, market risks, and the need to manage potential price or cash flow shocks.
- Changes in assumed asset lives or depreciation profiles should have a prospective impact: for example, the opening asset value prior to the change should be estimated on the basis of the previous depreciation assumptions.

6.4. Related-party transactions and transfer pricing

Related-party transactions are becoming increasingly common as utilities adopt more complex, and often more efficient, structures. The challenge for the regulator is to determine when two entities are related and what powers the regulator has with regard to related-party transactions, as well as the appropriate bases for cost allocation and pricing. The regulator's objectives will be the same as those that drive other aspects of regulatory accounting:

- obtaining better information on the costs of regulated monopoly services for future determinations,
- ensuring the equitable allocation of costs to regulated activities and unregulated activities,
- assessing the performance of the operator,
- improving the transparency of cost allocations and regulation, and
- protecting users against anticompetitive behavior.

Often, an operator will have a financial relationship with a related party. It may be as simple as sharing costs with a subsidiary providing unregulated commercial engineering or consumer services. Increasingly, however, relationships are more complex. The regulated operator may be part of a multisector company in which costs are shared across sectors, jurisdictions, and regulatory regimes. The regulated operator may pay a management fee to a holding company with diversified interests, or it may have structured itself as an asset-owning trust with a separate, unregulated service company managing the assets. Or a company may have put assets into a separate asset-owning trust in which the company owns as little as 20 percent of the shares but provides most of the management and operational services through a separate wholly owned subsidiary.

Such complex structures are becoming more common as competition is introduced into utility sectors and as utilities seek efficiencies through economies of scale or scope and placement of greater competitive pressures on their own activities. This makes dealing with related-party and transfer pricing more difficult. Without undermining incentives to improve efficiency, the regulator needs to ensure that the benefits of more efficient means of providing services are fairly shared and that no profit shifting or cost padding occurs.

Whether a regulator needs to incorporate related-party provisions in the accounting code is an open question. If the current structures are simple, the issues may be entirely academic, according to the materiality principle (see chapters 3 and 7), and no provision is necessary. This is more likely to be the case where the entity remains entirely in government ownership. In other cases, it will be impossible to avoid the issue, because the structures already exist, or the regulator may wish to provide greater certainty to operators for the future by anticipating the issues and providing clear guidelines.

Definition of related parties

Figure 6.1 illustrates some of the more complex structures that may exist and the transactions of interest to the regulator.

The definition of related parties is likely to focus on one or more of the following elements: ownership, control, and common economic interests.

Ownership can be quantified and clear rules can be set, but control and common economic interests are more nebulous concepts. U.S. Financial Accounting Board Standard 57 incorporates all three elements. Included in this standard are transactions between an entity and its principal owners, wherein a principal owner is defined as having more than 10 percent of the voting interest in the entity. The UK equivalent, Financial Reporting Standard 8 (FRS 8), does not specify a percentage ownership share in its primary definition, which focuses on the capacity to control or influence.[5] However, it does indicate that where a shareholder exercises control over 20 percent or more of the voting rights or where the entity is managed under a management contract, the regulator will assume that the entities are related, unless demonstrated otherwise.

Often, the existing structures may be simple, consisting of various wholly owned or majority-owned entities. In these cases, a simple definition based on ownership

Figure 6.1. Possible structures and relationships affecting a regulated entity

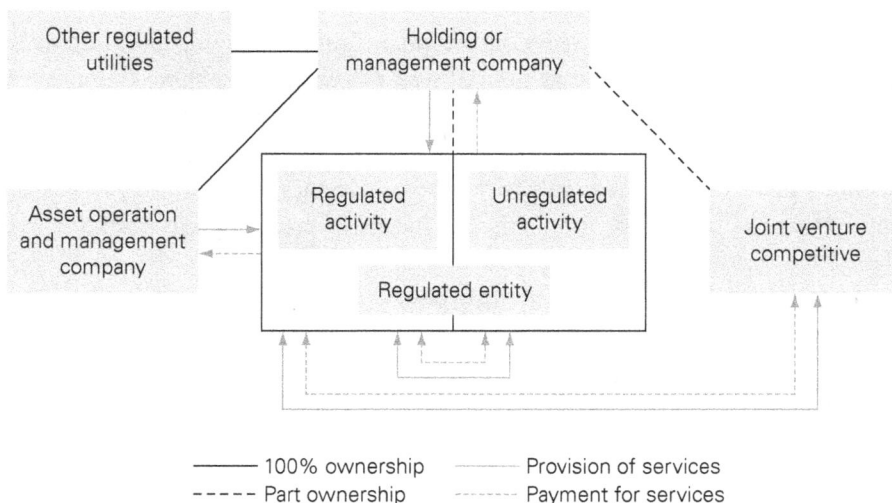

Source: Authors.

of a set percentage of voting shares may be sufficient. In other cases, more complex definitions may be required.

The UK energy and water regulators start from the definition of related parties in FRS 8. The Office of Gas and Electricity Markets (Ofgem) has modified FRS 8 so that if an entity is considered a related party of any company within the group, it is considered a related party of the regulated entity. Ofgem has a general power to deem any entity or person a related party (Ofgem 2002, 29).

In Australia, the Queensland and Victorian regulators adopted definitions based on whether an entity "has control or significant influence" over another entity (QCA 2003, 26–27). In a draft accounting code, the Independent Pricing and Regulatory Tribunal of New South Wales proposed a test based on common economic goals (IPART 2001, 7–8). The proposed interpretation of this test mirrored many aspects of the tests for control or influence under FRS 8, including the indicative 20 percent shareholding test.

Tests that rely on subjective judgments of control, influence, or common interests cope better with emerging structures, but they create challenges for the operator, because anticipating future obligations is difficult under different structures, and for the regulator, because subjective case-by-case decisions may be hotly contested.

Specified transactions

The regulator needs to specify the transactions of interest as well as the definition of related parties. The regulator may determine that all transactions between related parties are of interest, but this need not be the case. Some transactions may involve purchasing services at an arm's-length regulated price. For example, the engineering division may provide services at a customer's site on a competitive basis and as part of the service arrange for connection with its related utility. Other transactions may be too small to be of concern. Ofgem's requirements do not cover transactions with a total expected value of less than 0.25 percent of the regulated business turnover, or £500,000.

Table 6.4 classifies the types of transactions that may be involved and provides examples of those transactions.

Information disclosure

The accounting standards that apply generally to related-party transactions specify the requirements for disclosure and auditing of those transactions. Regulators have typically set similar, or more stringent, requirements for the disclosure of

6

Table 6.4. Types and examples of related-party transactions

Type of transaction	Examples	Issues
Service provider: unregulated associate **Service consumer:** regulated activity **Competition:** none in service provision	Gas services are provided by a local subsidiary of an international firm that funded the original bid and provides financial and management support. The subsidiary pays a management fee for this service.	Are the management fees reasonable relative to the costs and risks? What is a reasonable cost attribution? Are there comparators for these fees? What are the powers of the regulator in regard to these fees?
Service provider: unregulated associate **Service consumer:** regulated activity **Competition:** actual or potential competition	A gas distribution trust owns the network assets and is the regulated license holder but contracts out asset management and operation to a company that owns 30 percent of the trust.	Are the costs charged to the trust reasonable, or are they padded to transfer profits to the contractor? Is the contractor a related party? What are the regulator's powers? Are there benchmark prices? Was there competition to provide the services?
Service provider: regulated activity **Service consumer:** unregulated associate **Competition:** none in service provision	A regulated electricity utility gives access to its network assets and easements to a communications service joint venture in which it has a 50 percent interest.	Communication services are competitive but the input (access to network assets) is not. Although additional costs may be small, what share of the fixed costs should the communications activity pay for?
	A regulated gas distribution utility gives access to its pipes to its subsidiary for retail supply of gas.	If access is at standard regulated price, terms, and conditions, no issues arise.
Service provider: regulated activity **Service consumer:** unregulated associate **Competition:** actual or potential competition	The engineering staff of a regulated water utility provides advice to a joint venture bidding to build a water treatment plant outside the utility's monopoly territory.	Are the resources used properly tracked and costed? Is the price received comparable to competitive benchmarks? Does the revenue received exceed the costs incurred?

Source: Authors.

information on related-party transactions in regulated utilities. The regulator may require disclosure of the

- name of the related party involved,
- amount paid,
- services provided,
- method by which the price was determined (details of the cost allocation or market testing adopted), and
- means by which the transaction is reflected in the regulatory accounting statement.

Basis of cost allocation

The objectives in determining acceptable cost allocations or prices for related-party transactions are no different from those for transactions within the utility between regulated services and unregulated services. The regulator wants to be sure that the regulated utility pays no more than is reasonable for the services provided by related parties and is fairly compensated for services it provides to related parties. In principle, the same cost allocation and pricing methodologies that are deemed appropriate for internal transactions could apply to related-party transactions. In broad terms the regulator can specify the basis of the cost allocations from the operator and related parties for the services provided or compare the prices charged for the services with market benchmarks.

Specifying the basis of cost allocations is a common approach. As noted in chapter 4, several approaches to the allocation of costs are feasible. Although the regulator may find that it can specify cost allocation methodologies and information requirements when the regulated operator provides a service to a related party, its powers with regard to services provided by related parties to the regulated operator may be much more limited. For example, the operator may purchase management services from a related company that provides similar services to other companies within the group. Whether the regulator can request information on the cost allocations underpinning the services provided to the regulated operator depends on the powers its legislation provides.

Ofgem and Ofwat prefer to compare prices with market benchmarks wherever possible. Transfer prices are to be based on the market price, and market testing is to be used to establish the market prices for supplies. Where no market exists, transfer prices are based on costs allocated in relation to the way resources are consumed.[6] Many approaches can be used for market testing: competitive letting, comparison to published prices, third-party evaluation, and benchmarking. The problem is that for some services a service in the market may not be readily identifiable. An example may be a single-line contract for the management and operation of a water supply system.

In summary, specifying the requirements for transfer pricing and assessing the reasonableness of prices are among the most difficult challenges facing the regulator.

Additional reading and resources

Allen Consulting Group. 2003. "Principles for Determining Regulatory Depreciation Allowances." Note to the Independent Pricing and Regulatory Tribunal of New South Wales, Allen Consulting Group, Melbourne, Australia. www.ipart.nsw.gov.au.

IPART (Independent Pricing and Regulatory Tribunal of New South Wales). 2001. "Proposed Accounting Separation Code of Practice for Regulated Electricity Businesses in New South Wales." Issue 2, Section 3.4., IPART, Sydney, Australia. www.ipart.nsw.gov.au.

Ofwat (Office of Water Services). 2003. "Regulatory Accounting Guideline 1.03: Guideline for Accounting of Current Costs and Regulatory Capital Values." Ofwat, London. www.ofwat.gov.uk.

Notes

1. A common test for unfair competition through predatory pricing is whether the company is pricing at below marginal cost.

2. In many cases assets are built with excess capacity to allow for future growth and to avoid costly incremental additions to capacity. Optimization based solely on current use, or short-term expectations of use, may discourage efficient investment.

3. If the intangible asset, whether or not included in the rate base, has attained its value as a result of charges to ratepayers, revenue from its transfer should be imputed in a rate base.

4. *Roll forward* refers to the periodic adjustment of the regulatory asset base. Typically this adjustment will include the addition of capital expenditures less regulatory depreciation. If the asset base is measured in real terms, it may also be indexed or restated to depreciated replacement costs.

5. According to the Accounting Standards Board (1995, 7): "Two or more parties are related parties when . . .

- one party has direct or indirect control over the other party
- the parties are subject to common control from the same source

- one party has influence over the financial and operating policies of the other to the extent that the other party might be inhibited from pursuing at all times its own separate interests
- the parties, in entering a transaction, are subject to influence from the same source to such an extent that one of the parties to the transaction has subordinated its own separate interests."

6. Ofwat indicates that appointees are to demonstrate that a cross-subsidy does not exist, perhaps suggesting that a wide range of methodologies may be acceptable. A stand-alone or incremental cost allocation model can ensure that no cross-subsidies exist, and it could be argued that such a model reflects a view of relative resource consumption.

6

Chapter 7

Scope of a Regulatory Accounting System

For clarity and transparency, international best practice recommends that the regulator publish regulatory accounting guidelines summarizing the regulator's requirements, motivation, legal background, principles, and processes. These guidelines and the information they provide are discussed in the first major section of this chapter. Regulatory processes require utilities and possibly other stakeholders to provide substantial volumes of information over long periods of time. The processes and mechanisms, competencies, tools, and time and methodology required for this exchange are covered in the chapter's remaining sections.

7.1. Contents of regulatory accounting guidelines

Regulatory accounting guidelines (RAGs) usually include the following sections:

- purpose of the guidelines,
- legal basis and authorities,
- definitions of terms,
- general principles reflected in preparation of the guidelines,
- principles for preparing regulatory accounting statements, and
- information reporting requirements.

This chapter's annexes provide detailed templates for information reporting; pro forma documents; and detailed methodologies for revenue and cost allocation, asset valuation, calculation of cost of capital, and the like.

Purpose of regulatory accounting guidelines

RAGs define principles and directives to be followed by the regulated operator in preparing regulatory accounting. As described by the Essential Services Commission of Victoria (Australia; 2004), "The RAGs specify the Regulatory Body's requirements for the collection, allocation and recording of business data by the Regulated Operator and the reporting of that data to the regulatory Body."[1]

RAGs usually open with the principles underlying regulatory accounting: sustainability, productive and allocative efficiency, and equity (distributive efficiency). For example, infrastructure regulators in the United Kingdom (Ofgem and others 2001) commonly cite the following objectives:

- Monitor performance against the assumptions underlying price controls
- Detect anticompetitive behavior (unfair cross-subsidization and undue discrimination)
- Assist in monitoring the financial health of the operator
- Set prices
- Assist comparative competition (by promoting the submission of comparable information)

The first three objectives are essential in regulatory practice. The first two implicitly require an allocation of costs and revenues to

- verify that there is no discrimination among users of the regulated services,
- verify productive and allocative efficiency, and
- look for evidence of possible cross-subsidization of services.

Regulators can add other more general or specific objectives. One might be to improve transparency and help all parties to understand the regulator's information requirements and regulatory functions. Another objective might be to ensure that regulated operators report to the regulator on a timely, consistent, structured, and accurate basis.

Legal basis and authorities

The regulator's (independent body or ministry department's) rights and duties as defined by laws or decrees must be identified. By what legal authority is the regulator issuing guidelines? What are the regulator's powers of investigation, control, and auditing? The issue of the legitimization of the regulatory process is addressed in this chapter's last section.

Disclosure and confidentiality rules

A position should be taken on the following issues:

- What is the status of the information provided by the regulated operator to the regulator?
- What kind of information should be kept confidential, and in what circumstances (acknowledging that some information might be commercially sensitive)?
- Can the regulator eventually decide to disclose any kind of information if it thinks the information is in the public interest?[2]

RAGs should put in perspective the obligations of delivering regulatory accounting statements with other obligations imposed by law. For example, Essential Services Commission of Victoria (2004, issue 3, clause 2.3.5) states the following in its Electricity Industry Guidelines:

The Guidelines are minimum requirements. The obligation of a Licensee to comply with the Office's Guidelines—

- *Are additional to any obligation imposed under any other law applying to the Licensee's business; and*
- *Do not derogate from such an obligation.*

This last issue could be a source of confusion. The utility may be subject to other obligations (for example, general company legislation and corporate reporting) under other laws. These provisions make it clear that regulatory reporting provisions do not displace any other obligations and are not displaced by any other obligations under other laws. This issue is considered again in the context of the concept of *precedence*, which is examined below.

Revision, dates, and periods

RAGs should mention the following dates and periods:

- effective date of the RAGs' implementation,
- delivery dates (within "x" days of the end of the regulated company's financial year), and
- accounting periods to which the RAGs apply.

RAGs should acknowledge that they may be amended and expanded to meet the changing needs of interested parties. Therefore, they should state how these changes will occur and what process they will follow. Because transparency and consultation are key principles of all regulatory processes, it is advisable to create a working group to establish RAGs and to include the relevant professional accounting association in the process.

A good formal conceptual process is adopted in the above-noted Electricity Industry Guidelines. Whenever revising these guidelines, the Essential Services Commission of Victoria (2004) states that it will

1. state its intention;
2. call for input from industry participants and other interested parties;
3. have regard to that input, develop a draft, and publish it for comment by industry participants and other interested parties; and
4. have regard to the comments received on the draft, and develop and publish a revised guideline.

Definitions of terms

As is common in contract design, RAGs should provide accurate definitions of all terms they use.

General principles of preparation of the Regulatory Accounting Guidelines

Several general principles apply in preparation of RAGs.

General accounting and allocation principles

The general accounting and allocative principles most commonly listed in RAGs are causality, objectivity, transparency, consistency, and materiality.

- *Causality:* Costs, revenues, and capital should be allocated to the activities (services offered by the regulated operator) that cause those costs or revenues to arise (see chapter 4). The accounting system used by the regulated operator should allow verification of the causality between the amount taken into account and the activity (service). The Info-Communications Development Authority of Singapore (2001) states what, in practice, the regulated operator will need to do:
  - Review each cost and revenue item.
  - Identify the process that caused the cost to be incurred or the revenue to be earned (the driver).
  - Use the driver to attribute the cost or revenue to the relevant product or service and, accordingly, to the appropriate accounting separation segment.
- *Objectivity:* Allocation and valuation methodologies should not be designed in a way that benefits the regulated operator or any other party. This principle should

be applied to identification and treatment of costs to product, service, component, business, or disaggregated business.

- *Transparency:* The allocation methodology chosen by the operator should allow a breakdown analysis of the information for identifying types of costs, revenues, and capital. Where changes are made, the operator should restate the previous year's separate accounts on the new bases. Any change in accounting policies has to be explained in detail, and the effects have to be documented as well (in some cases, an authorization of the regulator will be needed before the change is implemented).
- *Consistency:* The bases of allocation of valuation should preferably be the same from year to year. Any change should be motivated and documented.
- *Materiality:* An item is considered material if its omission, misstatement, or non-disclosure has the potential to prejudice understanding of the financial position and nature of regulated business activities. To determine whether an item is material, the nature and the amount of the item should be assessed and compared to the regulated activity's basic financial figures, such as net worth, operating result, revenues, and costs. Some regulators, such as Ofwat (2002a), specifically mention a materiality threshold as a percentage of total income, costs, or profits.

Conformity of regulatory accounting with national accounting standards

RAGs should be considered obligations additional to any other general accounting obligations imposed by law (publication of statutory accounts).[3] RAGs usually require information that is not normally provided under a country's generally accepted accounting principles. Nevertheless, where applicable, regulatory accounting principles and policies should be adopted in compliance with national accounting standards.

Some guidelines also require an explicit reconciliation of general statutory accounts and regulatory accounts, which also serves the objective of comparability (Ofwat 2002a, clauses 3.4.2. and 3.4.3):

> *Where a Statutory Account amount has been consolidated or disaggregated in the Regulatory Accounting Statements, a worksheet must accompany the Regulatory Accounting Statements reconciling the Statutory Account amount shown in the Regulatory Accounting Statement to the Statutory Account amount in the Statutory Accounts of the Entity.*

> *The movement from Statutory Account to Regulatory Account will be clearly reported in the Regulatory Accounting Statements.*

RAGs should also address potential conflicts with national accounting standards and take a position on whether these standards or RAGS take precedence. In the

7

United Kingdom, a working group on the Role of Regulatory Accounts in Regulated Industries has indicated that RAGs should take precedence in the event of a conflict (Ofwat 2002a, footnote 1), whereas Ofwat's (1992, 2003a) RAGs state that "where the RAGs do not specifically address an accounting issue, then [UK] Generally Accepted Accounting Principles should be followed."

Substance to prevail over legal form

UK and Australian RAGs often state specifically that regulatory accounting statements should report the commercial substance of transactions. Where substance and form differ, the commercial substance rather than the legal form of a transaction or event shall be reported.

Related-party transactions and third-party benefits

The treatment of related-party transactions is likely to be one of the most difficult and controversial elements in the RAGs.

Related-party transactions. Related-party transactions (see chapter 6) occur between the regulated operator and legal entities affiliated with it (holding companies, branches, or subsidiaries of the same group) or commercially linked to it (through commercial agreements or common economic goals). The motivation for identifying these transactions separately is to allow the regulator to assess whether the transactions were recorded on a fair basis or under competitive conditions and to ensure that there was no unreasonable transfer of profits between the parties or between the operator's regulated activities and unregulated activities.

The Independent Pricing and Regulatory Tribunal (IPART) of New South Wales went into considerable detail in establishing the existence of related-party transactions (IPART 2001). First, IPART proposed to assess the regulated businesses independently of the legal structures used by the operators and bases its approach on the concept of common economic goals. It defined a *related party* as "any business that, operating with a Regulated Network Business or Regulated Retail Business, pursues objectives that are consistent with those of the regulated business (termed Common Economic Goals)" (IPART 2001). To establish the existence of common economic goals, several factors were proposed: ownership structure, options to purchase shares, control, decision-making capacity, economic dependence, intercompany loans and guarantees, and tax optimization. When related parties are different legal entities, IPART defined the existence of the relationship as the holding of 20 percent of voting rights or as the possibility of a party exercising "substantial influence over the policies and actions of the regulated business even though the influence is not based upon shareholding, shareholders, directors or officers" (IPART 2001).

Most regulators require that the principles and policies for trading between the regulated operator and related parties be documented. The regulator could even propose that the regulated operator adopt specific methodologies for "transfer pricing."[4] Regulators commonly use the following methodologies:[5]

- fully allocated costs,
- incremental pricing,
- prevailing market prices (through competitive tendering),
- tariff-based pricing,
- negotiated pricing, and
- asymmetric pricing.

Five methodologies are taken from the guidelines of the Organisation for Economic Co-operation and Development (1995):

- comparable uncontrolled price,
- resale price,
- cost plus,
- profit split, and
- transactional net margin method.

Third-party benefits. Transactions associated with subcontracting, purchasing, or other arrangements that cause the regulated operator or any related party to enjoy a materially beneficial interest in income or another value that accrues to a third party should be fully documented (value of transaction, description of arrangement and its purpose, details of involved parties, and so on).

Directors' responsibility

The regulator requires that the regulated operator attach a directors' responsibility statement to the regulatory accounting statement. This statement confirms that the regulatory accounting statement is fairly presented in accordance with RAGs and with regulatory and corporate legislation.[6] Typically, at least two directors of the regulated company sign and date the document.

Audit

The regulatory accounts provided by the regulated company will have to be audited (see chapter 5). Debate about who should audit the regulatory accounts is ongoing.

In most cases, the auditors of the regulated operator's statutory accounts will also audit the operator's regulatory accounts.

To verify compliance of the regulatory accounts statements with RAGs, the auditor must understand the regulatory framework and the obligations derived from the RAGs.[7] The audit should be conducted in accordance with the auditing standards in force in the country.

RAGs will specify the procedure for appointment and acceptance of the auditor (the auditor will have to be approved by the regulator).

The regulator can provide a pro forma regulatory audit report in the RAGs annex.

Principles for preparing the regulatory accounting statements

Regulatory accounting statements are derived from the statutory accounts (the regulated operator should reconcile the amounts from the regulatory accounting statements with the statutory accounts). The regulator will indicate how to treat items related to unregulated activities, consolidated amounts, and disaggregated items (which should be explicitly described in the "information requirements" section), as well as items related to separation of activities (such as production, transport, and distribution).

Cost and revenue allocation
Costs and revenues should be allocated to the different services from which they arise.[8] To allocate the different account items on a causality basis, the operator must identify one of the following relationships:

- a directly traceable cause-and-effect relationship with provision of the service;
- a verifiable relationship between the item and the output of the service; and
- a revenue or cost having a direct causal relationship with a pool of common costs or revenues and allocation of that pool on the basis of a relevant, reliable, and verifiable factor such as relative use.

Thus, regulated operators can attribute cost and revenues using the following categories:

- *direct or directly attributable revenues or costs* (revenues or costs solely generated by a particular service—for example, the cost of chemical products allocated to water production),
- *indirectly attributable revenues or costs* (revenues or costs that are part of a pool of common revenues or costs but that can be attributed to a particular service

through a nonarbitrary and verifiable cause-and-effect relationship—for example, the cost of a team that performs maintenance on assets belonging to different services), and

- *unattributable revenues or costs* (revenues or costs that are part of a pool of common revenues or costs and that cannot be attributed to a particular service, asset, or function through a nonarbitrary and verifiable cause-and-effect relationship—for example, administration or marketing costs).

Indirectly attributable revenues and costs will be allocated using an appropriate "driver." Nonattributable revenues and costs will be allocated using an appropriate factor.

Revision of methodologies
The regulator should make clear its right to change an allocation methodology that it considers does not meet its information requirements.

Qualification of costs
Qualification of costs could be a source of misunderstanding for operators unfamiliar with regulatory environments. Operators may not understand why some expenses, accepted from a statutory accounts or fiscal point of view, are not accepted by a regulator. The main reason is that the regulator bases its decision on an economic perspective and defends the interests of users. If the regulator judges, on a rational and motivated basis, that some costs are imprudent, unnecessary, or inefficient, it would deem recovery of these costs though tariffs paid by users (see chapter 5) to be economically inefficient and would exclude the costs from the calculation basis for future tariffs.

The rules for qualifying expenses proposed by the National Electricity Regulator of South Africa (NER 2002) are illustrative:

1. Expenses must be incurred in an arms'-length transaction; where possible suppliers are treated equally without prejudice.
2. Expenses must be incurred for the production and supply of electricity.
3. Expenses must be prudently incurred after careful consideration of available options.
4. Expenses must be incurred in the normal operations of the business. Where an expense is incurred under abnormal or extraordinary circumstances, consideration shall be given to spreading the expense over a number of years to match the time periods over which the benefit is derived.
5. The regulated entity shall have the onus to justify to the Regulator that the expenses incurred conform to the above criteria.

6. The regulator shall have the final discretion in allowing or disallowing an expense based on the above criteria.
7. Expenses on research and development, charitable donations, lobbying expenses and advertising may or may not be included, in part or as a whole, as part of costs of supply at the regulator's discretion.
8. The utility shall, in its price increase application, highlight all transactions with subsidiaries and sister companies.

Regulatory asset base

The regulator has to define the regulatory asset base (treatment of capital work in progress, inclusion of working capital, and the like). The regulatory asset base should include all assets necessary for efficient provision of the service. Long- or short-term financial investments, for example, will be excluded from the regulatory asset base.

The regulator must also define

- the cost accounting principles (current cost accounting, historical cost accounting, modern asset equivalent, market value; see chapter 6) to be used to determine asset values,
- depreciation policies for the regulatory asset base (see chapter 6), and
- its position toward revaluation of assets and goodwill or intangible assets.

The regulator should state that it has the ability to exclude some parts of the capital base of the regulated services if it considers that the parts are not necessary, efficient, or prudent.

Information (reporting) requirements

The information requirements section of RAGs defines the contents and structure of regulatory financial statements and repeats the accounting periods and delivery dates.

RAGs will impose a specific format of presentation. Ideally, the regulator provides the operator with an electronic worksheet each year for setting out detailed statements. The worksheet stores historical data and requests medium-term (usually five-year) projections of revenues, costs, capital expenditures, and other items (see this chapter's annexes for examples of reporting templates).[9]

RAGs will indicate the level of disaggregation of items as well as the main asset categories, activity areas, and cost categories. In addition, they will provide instructions on how to identify and treat specific items, such as customer contributions, tax effects, and related-party transactions.

Box 7.1. Ofwat's Regulatory Accounting Guidelines

The Office of Water Services (Ofwat), the economic regulator for the water and sewerage industry in England and Wales, lists the following documents in its RAGs:

- **RAG 1**: Guideline for accounting for current costs and regulatory capital values [version 1.03 of January 2003]
- **RAG 2**: Guideline for classification of expenditure regulatory acccunting guideline [version 2.03 of January 2003]
- **RAG 3**: Guideline for the contents of regulatory accounts [version 3.05 of January 2003]
- **RAG 4**: Guideline for the analysis of operating costs and assets [version 4.02 of January 2003]
- **RAG 5**: Transfer pricing in the water industry [version 5.03 of April 2000]

Source: www.ofwat.gov.uk (publication section).

The following is an example of a standard structure proposed for regulatory financial statements (Essential Services Commission 2004, issue 3): (1) profit and loss statement, (2) balance sheets, (3) revenue data (by tariff class and customer type, by region), (4) operating and maintenance expenditure, (5) capital expenditure, (6) fixed assets and depreciation (book values, tax values, regulatory values), (7) interest rates and borrowings, and (8) nonfinancial data (general operating statistics and indicators, technical, physical, commercial).

Box 7.1 provides a list of the RAGs issued by Ofwat.

7.2. Information exchange processes

Detailed information is required to ensure that

- operators do not earn excessively high or excessively low profits,
- operations are run efficiently (run with allocative and productive efficiency), and
- users and all participants in the sector are treated fairly.

This section focuses more specifically on information exchanges between the regulator and other parties, while also addressing relationships with the regulated operators (see figure 7.1).

Because its role is to defend the interests of all parties, the regulator can occupy a critical position in information exchange, but the regulator's precise role will depend on the design of the regulatory framework and methodologies. The regulator can play a credible and efficient role only in the following circumstances:

- Its role, rights, and obligations are legally defined and enforced.
- It is independent.
- It has the financial capacity and the specialized competencies to perform its role.
- It has clear and transparent processes for information exchange, validation of information, and dispute resolution.

The Utility Regulators Forum of Australia (1999) has listed nine best-practice regulation principles: communication consultation, consistency (across market participants and over time), predictability (reputation that facilitates planning by players) flexibility, independence, effectiveness and efficiency (cost-effectiveness emphasized in data collection and policies), accountability (clearly defined processes and rationales for decisions, with appeals), and transparency (openness of the process). Eventually, adherence to these principles will reduce the regulatory risk that figures in operators' perception of the cost of capital.

Figure 7.1. Information exchanges between regulator and regulated operators and other parties

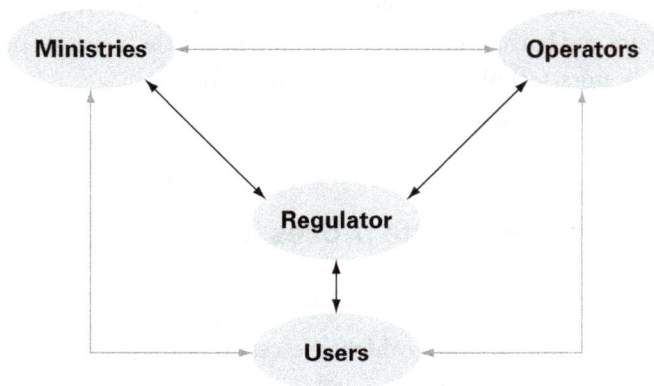

Source: Authors.

Institutional issues are not covered here, but it should be clear that the regulator should avoid political interference and that its role should be clearly defined.

Accountability, *communication and dissemination*, *consultation*, and *transparency* are key principles in information exchange.

Accountability

Information exchange processes have to be clearly defined, both the operator's obligations regarding the delivery of information and the regulator's obligations to operators and other involved parties (figure 7.2).

A formal process for communication and dissemination of information should include explicit deadlines, consultation periods, and dispute resolution processes.

Deadlines

Clear deadlines should be specified for

- formatted and scheduled information, x days after the end of the month, quarter, or year, depending on the nature of information;
- responses to questions, x days after question was raised;
- publication of main decisions; and
- reactions to consultation documents or final decisions.

Figure 7.2. Accountability of regulator and operator in the information exchange process

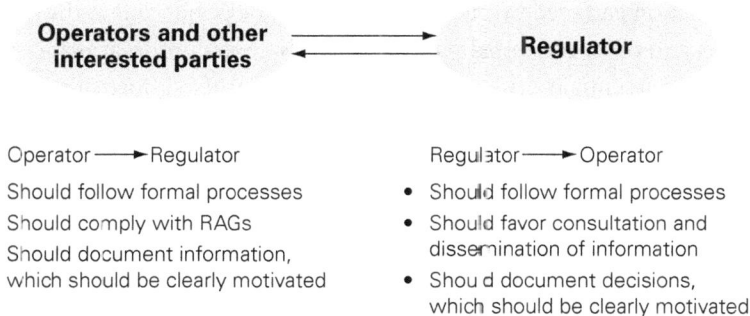

Operator ⟶ Regulator	Regulator ⟶ Operator
• Should follow formal processes	• Should follow formal processes
• Should comply with RAGs	• Should favor consultation and dissemination of information
• Should document information, which should be clearly motivated	• Should document decisions, which should be clearly motivated

Source: Authors.

Consultation period

During the consultation period, the various parties will have an opportunity to provide comments on the document made available for consultation by the regulator. The regulator will have to respond to each comment.

Dispute resolution

Disputes should be resolved in a reasonable timeframe.[10] Disputes can be resolved by litigation in court, arbitration, or alternate procedures (such as structured negotiations between parties; mediation involving a neutral third party; mini-trials with a hearing before a neutral legal adviser, such as a retired judge; or an expert determination). Arbitration and alternative dispute resolution procedures are common for managing conflicts for several reasons:

- Conflicts among operators, government, and regulators usually require considerable technical expertise. Compared with judges, arbiters with such expertise can be easier to find.
- Procedures (including the use of "fast track" mechanisms) are more flexible and convenient in arbitration and alternate dispute resolution than in national courts.
- Confidential information is better protected.

Applying appropriate dispute resolution procedures can save money and time. Procedures should be well designed, clear, simple, and transparent to all parties, and they should take place within a reasonable timeframe. Affordability is important. The expense of arbitration by international courts or organizations (in the millions of dollars) can penalize or discourage some parties.[11]

Communication and dissemination

The information gathered by the regulator should be public and at the disposal of consumers and other interested parties. The only constraint to availability should be specific confidentiality rules on commercially sensitive information or obligations derived from national information acts. (RAGs will address this matter and define criteria for confidentiality.) For dissemination of information, the regulator should use

- the Internet (to post reports, laws, decrees, resolutions, opinions, and decisions; see examples of electric utility Web sites in box 7.2),
- an open library on its premises, and
- public audiences and press conferences.

Box 7.2. Examples of utility regulator Web sites with substantial information

Europe
Ofwat (water, United Kingdom): www.ofwat.org.uk

Asia
Energy Regulatory Commission (electricity, Philippines): www.erc.gov.ph

Oceania
Independent Pricing and Regulatory Tribunal (multisector, Australia):
www.ipart.nsw.gov.au
Essential Services Commission (multisector, Australia):
www.reggen.vic.gov.au

Africa
Autorité de Régulation (multisector, Mauritania): www.are.mr
National Energy Regulator (electricity, South Africa): www.ner.org.za
Electricity Regulatory Board (electricity, Kenya): www.erb.go.ke
Commission de Régulation du Secteur de l'Electricité (electricity,
Senegal): www.crse.sn

Latin America
Brazilian Electricity Regulatory Agency (energy, Brazil): www.aneel.gov.br
Ente Nacional Regulador de la Electricidad (electricity, Argentina):
www.enre.gov.ar
Superintendencia Nacional de Servicios de Saneamiento (water and
sanitation, Peru): www.sunass.gob.pe
Organismo Supervisor de la Inversion en Energia (energy, Peru):
www.osinerg.gob.pe
Superintendencia de Servicios Sanitarios (water and sanitation, Chile):
www.siss.cl

Source: Authors.

Consultation

Interested parties should be allowed to participate in regulatory decisions. Use of discussion documents is recommended. When planning to take important decisions on major regulatory topics (regulatory regime, tariff determination, accounting

guidelines), the regulator should first seek the opinions of involved parties (operator, ministries, users associations) in consultation meetings. It should then draft a consultation document on the topic, which should be made public (through letters to parties and Web posting). Involved parties should have a specified period in which to comment on the document. The regulator should then make public all comments and its reactions. After a second round of reactions and possible adjustments, decisions can be taken or formally challenged. Figure 7.3 summarizes this process, and box 7.3 provides an example of the process for revision of a regulatory framework.

Figure 7.3. Regulatory decision-making process

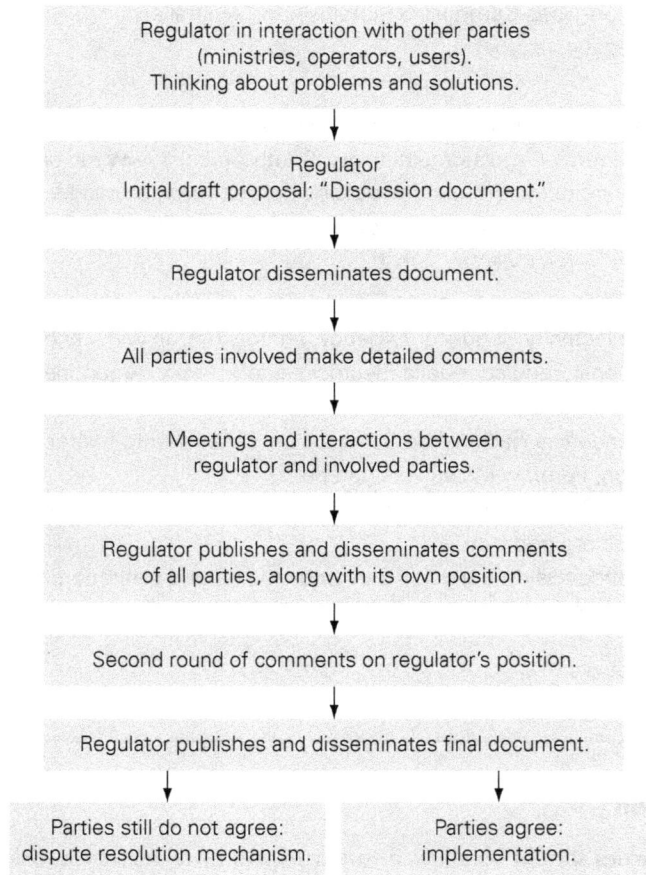

Regulator in interaction with other parties
(ministries, operators, users).
Thinking about problems and solutions.

↓

Regulator
Initial draft proposal: "Discussion document."

↓

Regulator disseminates document.

↓

All parties involved make detailed comments.

↓

Meetings and interactions between
regulator and involved parties.

↓

Regulator publishes and disseminates comments
of all parties, along with its own position.

↓

Second round of comments on regulator's position.

↓

Regulator publishes and disseminates final document.

↓   ↓

Parties still do not agree: Parties agree:
dispute resolution mechanism.   implementation.

Source: Authors.

Box 7.3. Example of consultation process: Revision of the regulatory framework for the economic regulation of the electricity supply industry of South Africa

Eskom dominates the electricity industry in South Africa. It supplies about 96 percent of South Africa's requirements. Eskom owns and controls the high-voltage transmission grid and supplies about 60 percent of electricity directly to customers; 177 local authorities (most of which purchase their energy and services from Eskom) supply the other 40 percent.

2001
National Electricity Regulator (NER) introduces a rate-of-return methodology to regulate the national electricity operator, Eskom. NER decides to refine its approach and prepares a proposal of detailed regulatory methodologies.

July 2002
NER produces the "Regulatory Framework for the Economic Regulation of the ESI [Electricity Supply Industry] of South Africa: A Discussion Document." NER later recognizes the document as "the first formal economic regulatory document in the history of the South African ESI" and as "a milestone in the development of robust regulatory methodologies for regulation in South Africa" (NER 2002).

August 2002
The document is approved for public comment by NER's board and is posted on NER's Web site. Comments are invited until December 2002.

December 2002
NER extends the deadline for comments to February 28, 2003.

February 2003
NER receives submissions from 11 organizations: Eskom, the Energy Intensive User Group, municipalities, PB Power, the Chamber of Mines of South Africa, and consultants.

May 2003
NER consolidates all comments in a summary document, "Summary of Comments of the Regulatory Framework for the Economic Regulation of the ESI of South Africa: A Discussion Document." It sends the document to stakeholders with an invitation to participate in a workshop to discuss the comments and to find "a consensus view on the most controversial issues."

Source: Authors.

7

Transparency

Clear rules add to the transparency of the process and reduce regulatory risk. In addition, they discourage any party from taking advantage of the weaknesses of a specific process to delay final decisions.[12]

7.3. Need for competencies, tools, and time and methodology

Analysis and validation of the operator's data and assessment of the operator's efficiency will likely require considerable interaction between the regulator and the operator. Clear rules for asking questions, exchanging comments, and taking decisions for tariff determination are required.

The large volume of data to record, process, and analyze will require competencies, tools, and time and methodology, each of which is discussed below.

Competencies

The regulator will have to analyze data of various types, including technical, financial, economic, social, environmental, and legal. This task will require assembling a staff with diversified skills, which may be difficult in developing countries. The organization of a regulatory authority is beyond the scope of this volume, but as a general principle, regulators should focus on issues that have a substantial impact on the rate of return of the concession and on efficiency and not on every management detail.[13]

Tools

Processing a large volume of data and information requires appropriate tools. Two are especially important: the economic-financial model and business information systems (knowledge database).

Models (see annex 2) are useful for tariff determination and arbitrage quantification, and the process of feeding the model with inputs will reveal any missing data.

Infrastructure concessions have a long life. During that time, the regulator will need to record and store crucial information of various kinds:

* historical data on operators;
* historical market data;

- contracts and annexes;
- laws, decrees, and resolutions related to the concession;
- regulatory guidelines;
- regulatory decisions; and
- all mail exchanged between interested parties, including comments, motivations, and justifications of issues raised.

Setting up an organized database with search engines on keywords will help regulators manage this information and preserve the knowledge.

Time and methodology

The regulator will have to process the data. As discussed above, regulation should be based on participation and collaboration, requiring time for the exchange of views, validation of key data and plans, and so on. Periodic tariff determination, in particular, requires years of advance work.

Consider Ofwat's 2004 periodic tariff review, a well-defined process that requires two years. Ofwat manages the review as a project requiring substantial resources from many stakeholders.[14] Figure 7.4 shows Ofwat's general planning for the tariff review. Box 7.4 provides details of Ofwat's planning process.

Ofwat's sophisticated procedures require substantial resources (time, money, competencies). Regulators in developing countries with few resources have to make their choices on the basis of their capacity, environment, and priorities. Nevertheless, their workload will be heavy, and major deadlines such as those for tariff determinations should be anticipated well in advance.

Figure 7.4. Ofwat's general planning schedule for tariff review

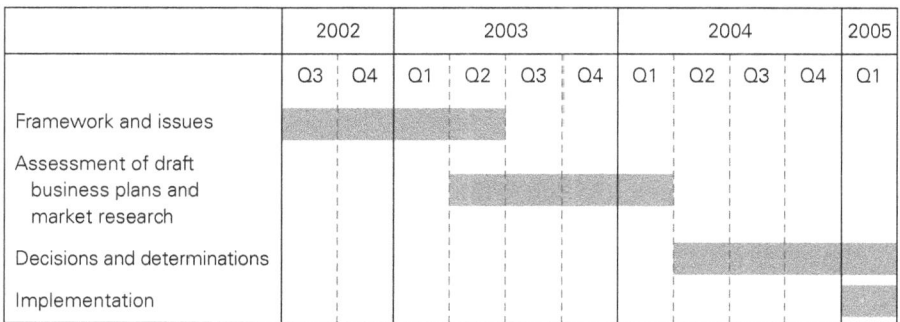

	2002		2003				2004				2005
	Q3	Q4	Q1	Q2	Q3	Q4	Q1	Q2	Q3	Q4	Q1
Framework and issues	███	███	██								
Assessment of draft business plans and market research				███	███	███	██				
Decisions and determinations								███	███	███	
Implementation											██

Source: Authors.

Box 7.4. Ofwat's 2004 tariff periodic review

The four phases in figure 7.4 are broken down into more detail here.

Phase 1: *Framework and issues*
Consultation on approach to review, input from ministries, and publication of results of negotiation:

- Oct. 2002: open consultation on Ofwat's approaches to the 2004 review
- Nov. 2002: market research stage 1 and publication of report
- Dec. 2002: receive initial guidance (on environmental and water quality improvement and social issues) from ministers
- Jan. 2003: consultation period ends
- March 2003: publish decisions on Ofwat's approach to the review
- May 2003: release update of financial model, issue draft business plan, publish feedback on cost base submissions (comparisons among operators made possible), confirm reference assumptions

Phase 2: *Assessment of draft business plans and market research*
Meetings with operators, annual reports, business plan proposals, feedback from regulator, and consultation with consumers' association:

- May–June 2003: Ofwat meets operators to prepare business plan
- June 2003: operators submit 2003–04 annual reports
- Aug. 2003: operators submit draft business plans
- Oct. 2003: publication identifies issues emerging from draft business plans
- Nov. 2003: Ofwat meets WaterVoice (consumers' association) to hear view on draft business plans
- Dec. 2003: operators receive details of 2005–06 programs; Ofwat publishes results of joint customer research
- Jan. 2004: ministers provide final guidance on the required quality program

Phase 3: *Decisions and determinations*
Final business plan, decisions project, annual reports, reactions from operators and users, publication of final tariffs, and final meetings with operators:

(continues)

Box 7.4. *(continued)*

- April 2004: operators submit final business plans
- June 2004: operators submit June returns, annual reports 2003–04
- July 2004: draft determinations published for consultation
- Sept.–Oct. 2004: ministers fine tune their decisions; Ofwat meets operators and other parties (points of view on determinations)
- Nov. 2004: Ofwat publishes final determinations
- Nov.–Jan. 2005: operators have two months to decide whether to accept or challenge price limits

Phase 4: *Implementation*

- March 2005: operators publish monitoring plans against which Ofwat will check progress annually
- April 2005: new price limits come into effect

Source: Authors.

7.4. Legitimizing the regulatory methodology

The regulatory methodology is a set of principles, rules, and processes that include

- regulatory objectives,
- the regulatory regime (rate of return, price cap, yardstick competition, hybrid),
- RAGs,
- topics related to tariff determination (determination itself, review dates, tariff structure, indexation formulas, cost pass-through, tariff stabilization mechanisms), and
- dispute resolution mechanisms for different categories of disputes.

This methodology should be legally enforced, whether in legislation or in the contract between the operator and the government (the regulator neither is nor should be a party to the contract).

Primary legislation (laws) is generally used to establish the broad framework of the infrastructure and to define the general objectives of the regulatory methodology. Secondary legislation (decrees, resolutions) is used for more detailed decisions.

The primary legislation should include principles similar to the four main regulatory objectives:

- financial sustainability (just and reasonable rate of return),
- allocative efficiency (prices reflecting costs),
- productive efficiency (minimization of costs over time), and
- equity (nondiscrimination).

Including more details of the regulatory methodology in the primary legislation could enhance the methodology's credibility or power, but the resulting loss of flexibility could increase the difficulty of implementing future changes. Thus details are preferably handled through secondary legislation or decisions of the regulator.

The regulatory methodology should be sufficiently enforced by (1) definition of the general principles in the primary legislation and (2) mentions in legislation or in the contract that the regulator will use regulatory tools such as models, define RAGs that should be applied by operators, and define processes for exchanging and validating information. The legislation should mention that regulatory decisions will be made after consultation with interested parties.

In brief, the foundation of the legal status of the regulatory methodology will always be the four main regulatory objectives, but to reinforce the practical implementation of that methodology, clear reference should be made in the legislation or the contract to tools and processes to be developed by the regulator.

Additional reading and resources

Essential Services Commission, Victoria. 2004. "Electricity Industry Guideline No. 3: Regulatory Information Requirements." Essential Services Commission, Victoria, Australia. www.esc. vic.gov.au.

NER (National Energy Regulator). 2002. "Regulatory Framework for the Economic Regulation of the Electricity Supply Industry of South Africa: A Discussion Document." Pricing and Tariff Department, NER, Pretoria. www.ner.org.za.

Ofwat (Office of Water Services). 2002. "The Review of Regulatory Accounting Guidelines: A Second Consultation Paper." Ofwat, London. www.ofwat.gov.uk.

———. 2003. "Regulatory Accounting Guideline 1.03, 2.03, 3.05, 4.02 and 5.03." Ofwat, London. www.ofwat.gov.uk.

Rosso, D. J., and C. S. Dorgan. 2002. "Arbitration and Dispute Resolution in the Electricity Industry." *Power Economics* 6 (6): 24–27.

Utility Regulators Forum, Australia. 2002. "National Regulatory Reporting for Electricity Distribution and Retailing Businesses." Discussion paper, Utility Regulators Forum, Melbourne, Australia.

———. 1999. "Best Practice Utility Regulation." Discussion paper, Utility Regulators Forum, Melbourne, Australia.

Notes

1. Formerly, the commission was the Office of the Regulator-General Victoria.

2. Information acts or other laws governing statistical information could serve as a guideline for treatment of confidential information.

3. Statutory accounts will usually include a company board's report, an auditor's report, a profit and loss account, and a balance sheet. Most countries authorize smaller companies to publish abbreviated reports. Public companies, quoted on a stock exchange, will usually face additional disclosure requirements.

4. IPART summarizes these methodologies and their use by regulators in appendix 3 of its "proposal of accounting separation code" (footnote 10).

5. For example, the National Association of Regulatory Utility Commissioners in the United States recommends the prevailing market price or the fully allocated costs methodology.

6. Most RAGs annex a pro forma statement to be used by the regulated operator.

7. Finding auditors with knowledge of utility regulations can be a problem in some developing countries.

8. The regulator and the regulated operator must clearly define the list of services (on the basis of a general separation of unregulated services from regulated services and a disaggregation of the latter).

9. In the Argentine gas sector, the information sent by the companies to the regulator has the status of a sworn affidavit. Companies have two months to send any revisions, and after that the information is taken as final. Errors or misrepresentation can result in fines (which are clearly stated in the rules).

10. This section is based on Rosso and Dorgan (2002).

11. The International Chamber of Commerce (ICC) in Paris, for example, is used as an arbiter in many concession contracts (see www.iccwbo.org/index_court.asp).

12. An operator could attempt to take advantage of a political situation (election year, change of staff of the regulatory authority) that might favor its position, or a regulator or government could attempt to take advantage of coming changes in the business strategy of the operator's group.

13. For more detail on this topic, see Smith (1997), Kerf and Geradin (2000), and Kerf (2000).

14. See "Timetable for 2004 Periodic Review" (www.ofwat.co.uk).

Understanding Financial Statements: Ratio Analysis

Accounting is aimed at recording all of a firm's economic facts, but it implies more than financial statements. Analysis of the information in these financial statements can identify key relationships and trends underlying the firm's economic and financial performance. Stakeholders interested in the company's business (shareholders, investors, credit institutions, staff) can use the branch of accounting known as "analysis and interpretation of financial statements" to assess the company's performance across periods (horizontal analysis) or against other businesses or sectors (vertical analysis) when they engage in investment, financial, and business decision-making processes.

The most widely used technique in the analysis of accounting and financial data is ratio analysis, which provides insight into a specific aspect of the firm's performance that may be related to the firm's liquidity, activity, capital structure, or profits and profitability.

In addition, financial analysts generally use two criteria to assess the reasonability of a financial ratio: a trend analysis, to assess performance over time, and a vertical analysis, to compare the company's financial ratios with those of similar businesses or industry averages. In a trend analysis, the macroeconomic context of the company's business is an important consideration—for instance, businesses often operate with less liquidity in a high-inflation context than in a more stable situation—because this element may bias an indicator's interpretation over time. In trend analysis and vertical analysis, the ratios are meaningful only when compared with reference points, whether of other periods or with the levels found in other businesses in the same or a similar industry.

Liquidity ratio analysis

Liquidity analysis concentrates on the short run, for no longer than a year's time from each year-end. Financial ratios in this category measure the ability of a company to meet its current obligations as they come due. These obligations are part of the company's liabilities and, in general, they exceed the company's cash resources.

Current ratio

The money to meet the company's current liabilities is generated from the company's current assets—out of the company's own liquid reserves, plus temporary investments, plus accounts receivable and inventories. One of the first measures of liquidity is this current or global liquidity ratio, which is calculated with the following formula:

Current ratio = current assets / current liabilities.

This ratio shows the number of monetary units of current assets that finance each unit of current liabilities. A ratio below 1 is usually evidence of difficulties. A much higher value does not necessarily indicate a positive situation; it might be evidence, for instance, that the firm is giving large credits to its customers.

Acid test

Like the current ratio, the acid test is a static index. It is calculated at year-end, although from a more restrictive point of view than the current ratio. The acid test indicates the company's immediate ability to pay its debts, which strongly indicates its liquidity. The acid test ratio is calculated as follows:

Acid test = (cash + temporary investments + accounts receivable) / current liabilities.

A value near 1 means that the company can meet its current liabilities with its available assets or assets readily convertible into cash.

Activity ratios

Activity ratios represent a measure of operative efficiency in the use of a company's resources.

Accounts receivable turnover ratio

The ratio of accounts receivable to turnover shows the number of days it takes customers to pay their bills. The greater the number of days, the higher the delinquency rate seen in customers' payment habits. The lower the number of days, the better for the company, because its resources will not result in idle investments in accounts receivable, which usually generate a low rate of return. The accounts receivable turnover ratio is calculated as follows:

Accounts receivable turnover = accounts receivable / daily credit sales,

where daily credit sales is calculated as

Daily credit sales = net credit sales per period / days in period.

The collection term may vary from company to company, depending on trading practices. Thus, a typical collection term in sales conditions would be 30 days, although this term depends on the industrial sector in which the company operates. A higher ratio for accounts receivable may indicate a problem with the company's credit policy. In addition, it may imply that the company is competitively weak and, therefore, that it needs to offer longer collection terms.

A1

Inventory turnover ratio

The inventory turnover ratio indicates the time it takes to sell inventory—that is, the time before the goods are converted into cash. This ratio is calculated in the following manner:

Inventory turnover = (cost of goods sold / average inventory).

To assess whether the resulting ratio is appropriate, analysts should compare it with another company in the same industry. If the ratio is too high, it may be evidence of a low inventory turnover, which might result in lost sales. A low ratio could be evidence of inventory obsolescence, which will clearly depend on the sector in which the company operates.

Accounts payable turnover ratio

The accounts payable turnover ratio indicates the time it takes the company to meet its obligations. This ratio is calculated as follows:

Days in accounts receivable = accounts payable / daily cost of goods sold.

The daily cost of goods sold is calculated as follows:

Daily cost of goods sold = cost of goods sold / days in period.

If the number of days the company takes to pay its accounts payable exceeds the ordinary credit terms (for instance, 30 days), the company may be too confident in suppliers' attitudes and may lose the discounts available for prompt payment, though the right value of this ratio will generally depend on the sector of the industry in which the company does business.

Capital structure (leverage ratios)

Capital structure ratios measure the relative position of equity owners compared with that of a company's lenders. One such ratio is the debt-to-equity ratio, measured as follows:

Debt-to-equity ratio = total liabilities / owners' equity.

This ratio measures the combination of funds in the company's net worth financial situation (funds-financing assets) and is used to compare the capital invested by the company's owners (shareholders) with the funds provided by lenders. As a general rule, the higher the ratio, the greater the risk that the company may experience difficulties in repaying loans and meeting its liabilities.

No general agreement on an adequate value for this ratio exists, but in general a value higher than 1 is considered risky. However, if a company generates profits and has relatively stable cash flows, such a value may be considered acceptable, whereas it would not be for a firm with highly volatile profits. Typical debt-to-equity ratios vary substantially among industries, and ratios above 1 are more common in the utility sectors, in which business risk is comparatively low.

The debt-to-equity ratio is often used together with an indicator called *interest coverage,* which alerts analysts when net interest (if negative) starts to represent a significant part of a company's profits.

Profits and profitability

Profitability ratios are used to measure management's ability to generate profits and to analyze their relation with the company's overhead. Although various indicators are used to measure profitability, this section presents the ones most frequently obtained from a company's financial statements.

Gross margin ratio

The gross margin represents the difference between sales and the cost of goods sold; it is calculated as follows:

$$\textit{Gross margin ratio} = \textit{gross margin} \,/\, \textit{total sales.}$$

This ratio expresses the extent to which profits depend on a company's operations. An increase of the gross margin means that the company is more efficient—that the share of sales represented by its costs is decreasing.

Net margin

The net profit ratio shows the share of the company's sales that is turned into profits. This ratio is calculated as follows:

$$\textit{Net profit margin ratio} = \textit{net profit of fiscal year} \,/\, \textit{total sales.}$$

In general, the higher this indicator, the more efficient the company is in producing and selling goods and services.

A1

Return-on-assets ratio

The return-on-assets ratio, widely used in corporate finance analysis, enables evaluation of management's ability to generate a reasonable return on assets, regardless of whether the assets were financed by debt or equity. Investment opportunities for the company's capital are many; therefore, obtaining the best return possible, according to the appropriate commercial risks, is necessary. The most commonly used calculation formula is the following:[1]

Return on assets % = (net profit of fiscal year / average total assets × 100).

This indicator is highly sensitive to the capital requirements of each sector. Therefore, comparison of this indicator for businesses in the same industry sector is recommended.

Return-on-equity ratio

The return-on-equity ratio considers only the return obtained by management on shareholders' investment (owners' equity) rather than on the whole company's capital, as with return on assets.

"Return" for shareholders is the business's net profit. Therefore, return on equity is calculated as follows:

Return on equity % = (net profit before taxes / average owners' equity × 100).

A high return on equity implies high prices for the shares of stock, which not only eases the capture of new funds, but also puts the company in a better condition to grow.

Note

1. Analysts commonly assume that calculation of net profits takes into account the tax shield generated by interest payment.

Regulatory Model

This annex provides an introduction to the design and uses of financial and economic models to quantify transparently the impact of regulatory decisions. It draws on the lessons from developed countries and developing countries in ordinary and extraordinary revisions in the context of contract renegotiations.

The most effective regulators in developing countries follow remarkably similar approaches. They essentially rely on UK-type regulatory processes adapted to local constraints and concerns. The main common element is use of relatively simple quantitative models of operators' behavior and constraints to measure the impact of regulatory decisions on some key financial and economic indicators of concern to operators, users, and government.

To simplify, these models force regulators to recognize that, in the long run, private operators need to at least cover their opportunity cost of capital, including the various types of risks specific to the country, sector, and projects in which they are involved. Because these variables change over time, revisions that allow adjustment in the key determinants of the rate of return for the operator are needed. These revisions must reflect recognition that all tariffs, subsidies, quality, investments, and other service obligations are interrelated, and that they jointly determine the rate of return. At every revision, the rules of the game for the regulator are exactly the same: figuring out the changes in the cost of capital and adjusting the variables driving the rate of return to ensure that it remains consistent with the cost of capital.

These models have to be based on sound data collection processes for each of the key decision indicators. If the models can draw on reasonable data, they do everything any financial model would do for day-to-day management of a company, as

---

This annex is drawn from Estache and others (2002).

well as take a longer-term view and explicitly identify the key regulatory instruments. They can help regulators monitor the consistency between cash flow generated by the business, on the one hand, and debt service and operational expense needs, on the other, to address the main concerns of operators. They can also account for many key policy factors, including access and affordability concerns for various types of consumers. They generally account for the sensitivity of operators and users to various regulatory design options.

What are regulatory models?

Regulatory models are essentially "improved" financial models designed to provide a rigorous analytical tool to allow regulators to address their most predictable concerns in a consistent way. They calculate the internal rate of return (just as a financial model would), accounting for all contractual constraints imposed on operators. In particular, they allow the regulator to account for social concerns and for the behavior of the various agents (users, operators, and government). They also allow for simulation of consequences for agents of any policy or behavioral change.

However detailed these regulatory models may be, they all follow a similar structure (summarized in figure A2.1). They build on an initial database (summarizing the company's physical and financial performance, including most of the accounting information regularly collected by the operator), an identification of the main regulatory instruments (for example, tariff structure, quality options, and investment speed and timing), and some economic parameters (for example, demographic characteristics of the area of operation, macroeconomic indicators driving demand, and efficiency levels).

Next, they rely on explicit assessments of the expected impact on cash flows of the reaction of the main actors (users and operators) to the regulatory instruments summarized analytically. This reaction is reflected in the regulatory models through incorporation, for example, of the relationship between consumption levels and prices. Assessment of the reaction drives the financial equilibrium for the operator (this assessment can be performed on a fairly detailed level for the main categories of costs and revenue).

Once the regulator has a good assessment of the operator's situation based on a relatively large set of performance indicators, and depending on the specific regulatory regime (price cap, profit sharing, or rate of return) selected, it can determine

A2

Figure A2.1 Building Blocks of Regulatory Models

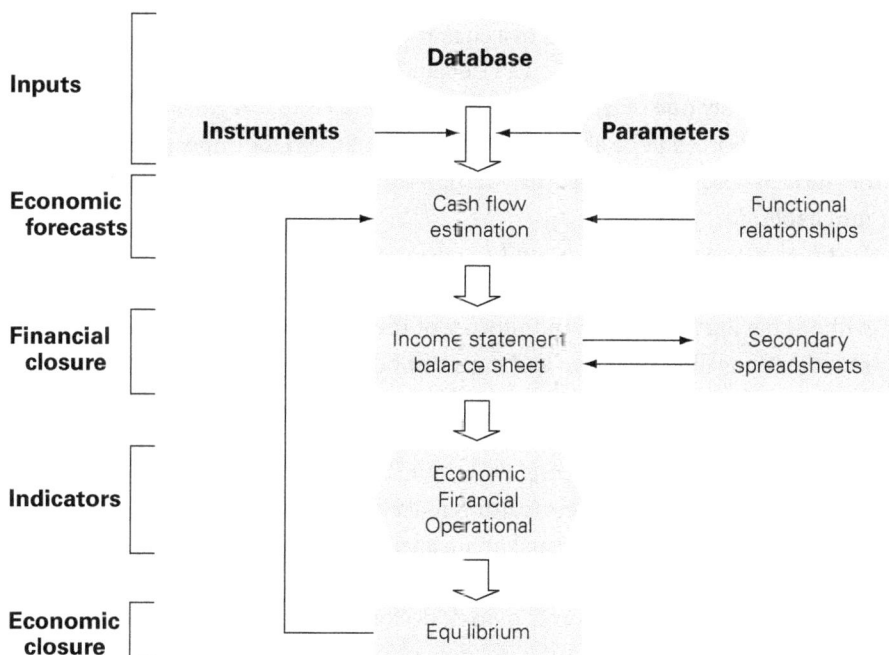

Inputs

Economic forecasts

Financial closure

Indicators

Economic closure

Database

Instruments → ← Parameters

Cash flow estimation ← Functional relationships

Income statement balance sheet → ← Secondary spreadsheets

Economic Financial Operational

Equilibrium

Source: Authors.

the revenue that the operator will be allowed to collect though its tariff. The equilibrium tariff is the one that generates a net present value of zero for the investment or the operation. This assessment is driven by the cash flow forecast, which is built into the forecasted income statement of the operator through a complex set of secondary spreadsheets. These spreadsheets are used to generate the main monitoring indicators on which a regulator needs to focus. Once these indicators are acceptable, the final average tariff is known. "Negotiations" between operators and regulators usually require several rounds until agreement is reached or until the regulator decides to stop them, but in each round the process is exactly the same.

This generic definition can be complemented by a brief summary of the contributions of regulatory models to implementation of regulatory policies:

- *Quantitative rigor in regulatory assessments:* Regulatory models allow regulators to avoid subjective or impressionistic assessments of the impact of their decisions. What should be the impact of a devaluation on a tariff? This question

A2

requires an understanding of a company's financial structure (how much foreign debt it includes) and that understanding must have a quantitative basis. What is the impact on the tariff of a change in the country risk premium between two tariff revision periods? No less demanding in terms of numbers, this question is probably one of the most common questions that regulators in developing countries need to be able to answer. Without the rigor imposed by the kinds of models presented here, the responses to these questions are at best unreliable.

- *Distinction between economic and financial concerns:* Regulatory models allow regulators to account for the financial and accounting concerns of operators without having to abandon monitoring of the wider concerns of society. Investment decisions by operators and consumption decisions are endogenous. The models recognize that regulators may have to account for social concerns. They are designed to assess the trade-offs between types of resource allocation problems. They can also provide useful input into the fiscal budgetary process when subsidies are needed. All these features make them more appropriate to the regulator's concerns than traditional financial models, but without quite fully being economic models. They can be labeled "quasi-economic" models, because they still fall short of what economic models do for policy makers. For instance, they rely on market prices rather than shadow prices, and ignore externalities such as the environmental effects of operations and any other distortions of factor or product markets.

- *Consistency in accounting for multiple concerns:* Regulatory models force consistent quantification of the financial and (quasi-)economic viewpoints of regulatory decisions. From a financial perspective, the regulator is asked to focus on synthetic indicators, such as the cost of capital and the internal rate of return or equivalent concepts, and to understand the trade-offs of various regulatory or policy instruments in terms of their impacts on these indicators. How will a government's request to revise a contract in terms of investment levels or speed influence the profitability of the business? How should tariff levels be adjusted to restore the original profitability? Only a model that recognizes all the interactions of the various decision variables can answer these questions.

From an economic perspective, the main concern of the regulator is to ensure continuity of services, to achieve various types of efficiency (cost and resource allocation minimization while ensuring that prices are consistent with costs), and to meet political mandates in terms of any social and redistributive concerns. One sort of social concern that policy makers and regulators must be able to address is consistency of a tariff adjustment authorized to compensate for an unexpected change in macroeconomic conditions with the poorest users' ability to pay. Policy makers have not always clarified their policy preferences, and there may be policy options (for example, explicit payments or vouchers) that can better address their concerns. Policy makers' lack of action or direction on social issues places regulators in a difficult position; they have not always met the challenge of simultaneously accounting for multiple variables. In many of these failures, the main victims are the people least capable of arguing their case. In practice, these victims are often the poorest users. Social concerns often are inadequately addressed through social policy and often are left out of the regulatory decision-making process.

- *Transparency and accountability:* Regulatory models are crucial in increasing transparency in monitoring of the behavior of regulators and operators. They reduce the scope for corruption and collusion, the cost of which they capture or at least significantly increase. They facilitate the job of watchdogs to ensure that no abuses occur and that the expected gains from reform are indeed achieved and shared with users. By increasing the transparency of the factors driving the operator's allowed rate of return, ensuring that it covers the company's expected cost of capital until the next tariff revision, and by increasing the transparency of the factors increasing the operator's cost of doing business, the models provide a regulatory tool for organizing consultation processes.

  Regulatory models will not alleviate the need for discussion. In fact, public hearings are organized to elicit input on the main elements to be addressed by the models and to allow all actors to intervene. Ultimately, however, the regulator will have to decide most matters on objective, technical grounds rather than on subjective, political grounds. The former make regulation fairer, more efficient, and less amenable to political interference or corruption.

Even the best regulatory models are by necessity simplifications of the interactions they represent. The quality of a model depends, among other factors, on the strength of assumptions about future costs and investment requirements, growth in demand, the consumption profile of users, and the ability of the operator to improve its efficiency. How good these assumptions are, in turn, depends on the quality of the data available. Regulators should never forget that the data they need must match the goals of the model. The regulator must always arbitrate between the costs and benefits to the operator and users of generating additional information. In many countries the information available is so limited that the initial assumptions have often been quite broad. As time goes by, the information asymmetry between regulators and operators shrinks, and narrower assumptions are needed. Unlike the operator's financial department, regulators need not be concerned with weekly or monthly monitoring. Their focus is on the medium to long run, and hence their data requirements are likely to be lower.

Matching regulatory objectives and instruments

Most regulatory regimes attempt to meet multiple objectives. Their ranking varies across countries, and in many instances trade-offs are unavoidable. A few of these objectives appear to dominate. The regulatory challenge then becomes the need to consider various instrument combinations as a way of simultaneously meeting primary and secondary objectives or at least of minimizing the need to face socially and politically difficult trade-offs.

Regulatory objectives

The main objectives quoted by regulators are as follows:

- *Financial viability of the operator:* Ultimately, if tariffs (including subsidies) do not cover costs, private operators are not interested. Most companies are willing to be in the red for a couple of years early on when they take over the business, but only for the short run. The related indicators are the internal rate of return and the net present value.
- *Productive efficiency:* This goal reflects the concern to push operators to minimize costs for a given level of production or to maximize production for a given level of inputs. A problem with rate-of-return regulation is that it does not promote cost minimization. A benefit of price or revenue caps is that, when effective, they tend to improve productive efficiency. Related indicators are production or coverage levels for given expenditure levels on inputs, or vice versa.
- *Allocative efficiency:* This goal reflects the need to ensure that tariffs reflect marginal cost. Yet distortions in factor markets, limited credit markets, unionized labor, and complex tax systems are completely out of the regulator's control. Related indicators reflect changes in the input or output mixes as a result of changes in input or output prices.
- *Dynamic efficiency:* This relatively subtle goal is to ensure that the operator has an incentive to think of future users and to invest accordingly. This goal reinforces

A2

the importance of ensuring that tariffs cover costs, including the cost of investments needed for future users. Related indicators establish a link between demand forecast and current investment levels.

- *Distributional fairness*: This goal implies that tariff structures per user type are consistent with ability to pay. When government cannot credibly commit to subsidies, regulators often rely on cross-subsidies to help the poorest users. Providing these users with additional, cheaper technologies is another way to achieve fairness. One indicator of affordability is the percentage of income spent on the services classified by income groups. Trade-offs between objectives—such as between sustainability and efficiency, between efficiency and fairness, and between sustainability and fairness—are many.

- *Sustainability and efficiency:* The regulator needs to strike a balance between marginal cost pricing and exclusion of inefficient costs, which may promote allocative and productive efficiency, and preservation of the financial sustainability of service provision. Variations in financial conditions mean that this problem is not static. At every tariff revision, the regulator will have to ensure that prices are consistent with the need to recognize the consequences of fluctuations in global financial markets on the operator's financial viability. The balance between price and market fluctuations is particularly important in countries in which long-term borrowing capacity is limited because of the weakness of credit markets. Most borrowing is short term, and hence short-term fluctuations have immediate impacts on the financial state of the operator. This needs to be reflected in the average level of prices just as much as the concern for efficiency revealed by the usual emphasis on long-run marginal cost pricing.

- *Efficiency and fairness:* There are two main types of trade-offs. The first is between efficiency, on the one hand, and price discrimination in favor of the poor to address equity concerns, on the other hand. Cross-subsidies have long been criticized for inefficiency. When the ability of the government to finance direct subsidies is limited, cross-subsidies may be unavoidable, but different subsidy designs will have different efficiency effects. The second trade-off is between the extent of and quickness with which users benefit from efficiency gains, on the one hand, and the incentive of the operator to maximize these gains, on the other hand. The strength of the incentive for firms to cut costs is related to the share of the savings they are allowed to appropriate. If all gains must be passed on immediately to users, firms have no incentive to cut costs. At the other extreme, allowing a firm to keep all efficiency gains achieved in delivery of a monopolistic public service is both socially and politically unrealistic. Efficiency gains eventually must be shared with users through a combination of lower tariffs and better service quality.

- *Sustainability and fairness:* Historical subsidy levels may not be consistent with the desire to guarantee financial viability to the operator. The transition from public to private provision of public services often implies a review of many historical subsidy levels and designs tolerated under soft budget constraints for public enterprises. Once a private operator takes over, the cost of subsidies becomes a more serious issue, and the concern for financial sustainability forces the regulator to rethink subsidy levels and structures. The "privatization" process thus may force decisions on politically sensitive trade-offs.

The existence of these trade-offs and the related political sensitivities imply that regulatory regimes must fit into more formal processes to ensure their political acceptance and long-run sustainability. Where the regulator is required to make trade-offs, these trade-offs should be transparent, and the regulator should be accountable for its choices. Regulatory regimes must be simple, justifiable and justified, transparent, acceptable to the majority of actors, and fair in the allocation of total costs. Moreover, they must avoid unjustified price discrimination as well as excessively fluctuating price levels. Models such as those described here are not merely instruments for checking quantitative consistency: they are the key to accountable and acceptable processes that ensure the long-run viability of reforms. The transparency achieved through use of models is particularly important when trade-offs between objectives have highly differentiated consequences for different interest groups.

Regulatory instruments

To achieve a particular combination of regulatory objectives, the policy maker or regulator has many instruments from which to choose, as illustrated in figure A2.2. These instruments can be aggregated into three broad categories:

- regulatory regime,
- contractual obligations, and
- tariff level and design.

A distinctive feature of regulation is that these instruments are interrelated through their financial impact on the firm.

Figure A2.2 Main Policy Instruments for Regulators

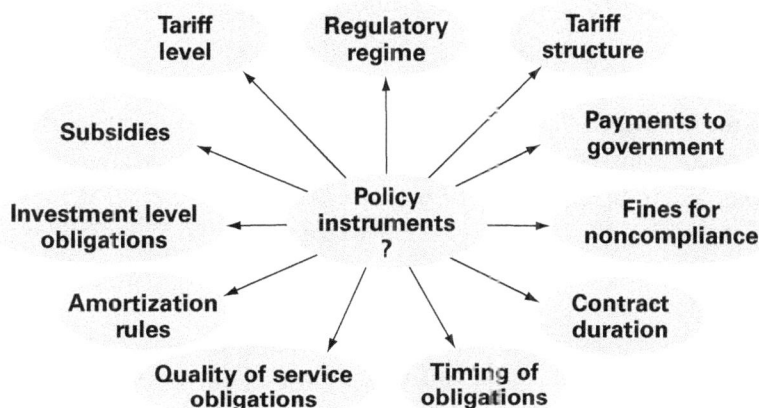

Source: Authors.

The relation between the various goals and instruments is reasonably close and can be summarized as in table A.2.1.

It should be clear by now that the average tariff level drives the operator's financial sustainability. The tariff should allow an efficient firm to cover its cost and achieve a reasonable rate of return. If the tariff does not cover costs, subsidies will be a complementary option. But the design of subsidies may have an impact on allocative efficiency, because subsidies change relative prices. In highly unpredictable markets, the regulatory regime drives the incidence of the level of risk on tariff levels. Price caps in highly volatile environments, combined with excessively spaced tariff revisions, may result in financial unsustainability for the operator.

Table A2.1 Regulatory Goals and Instruments for Their Achievement

Goals	Instruments
Sustainability	Tariff levels and subsidies; regulatory regime
Allocative efficiency	Tariff structure
Productive efficiency	Regulatory regime (sharing of efficiency gains)
Fairness	Tariff structure; service obligations (e.g., investment levels and service quality); regulatory regime (sharing of efficiency gains)

A2

149

Within regulated activities, allocative efficiency is influenced essentially by the tariff structure. Unless the structure is closely (negatively) related to the demand elasticity of the various users, allocative efficiency is distorted. Tariff structures may reflect social concerns, revealing a major trade-off between these concerns and allocative efficiency.

Next, the tariff level allowed for sustainability must be consistent with the desire to achieve productive efficiency—that is, to authorize only the recovery of efficient costs. The design of the regulatory regime essentially determines the operator's incentive to minimize costs. Price or revenue caps that are set for a specified period (for example, five years) are more likely to achieve productive efficiency than yearly cost-based adjustments.

Finally, fairness is clearly associated with the design of the tariff structure because, in addition to subsidies, the tariff structure is the main mechanism used to match prices with ability to pay. The regulatory regime also matters, but in a more subtle way, because the effect of the level of risk on tariff levels is driven by the regulatory regime. In a highly volatile environment, a cost-plus regime with frequent adjustments can result in frequent large changes in prices. But if these risks are borne by the operator under a medium-term price cap, they will need to be reflected in the cash flow modelling or allowed cost of capital.

What regulators need to know about the operator's finances

Ultimately, what the regulator does is identify a tariff level that will generate a cash flow consistent with valuation of the firm. That tariff level must be consistent with the firm's opportunity cost of capital. In other words, the regulator needs to focus on two main groups of indicators: the cost of capital, which is a hurdle rate to decide whether a tariff level is reasonable, and the firm's cash flows, which are used to assess the firm's internal rate of return. The ideal regulatory situation is one in which the tariff is set so that the internal rate of return of a project or concession is equal to the cost of capital. For the project to be attractive to a private operator, the internal rate of return must be at least equal to this cost of capital. When the cost of capital is higher than the internal rate of return, the net present value of the project is negative.

Figure A2.3 depicts key factors driving cash flows and hence the internal rate of return. The figure illustrates the reality that operators and regulators do not drive

Figure A2.3 Drivers of the Internal Rate of Return

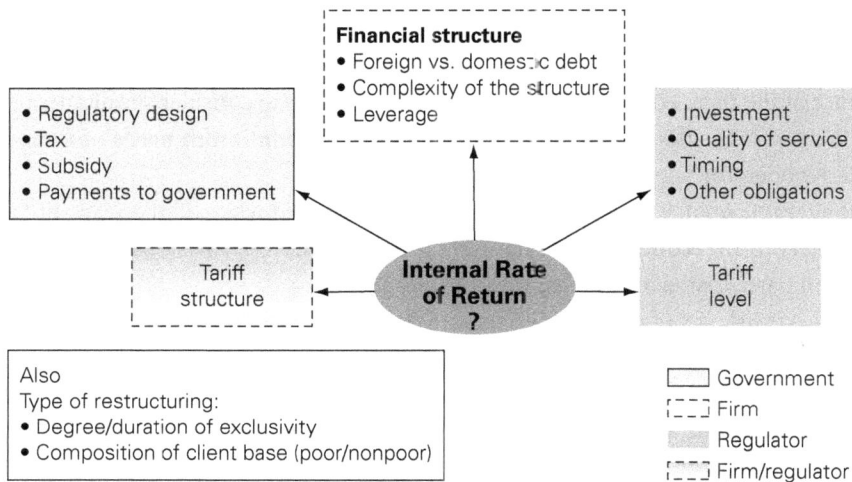

```
┌ ─ ─ ─ ─ ─ ─ ─ ─ ─ ─ ─ ─ ─ ─ ─ ─ ─ ┐
  Financial structure
  • Foreign vs. domestic debt
  • Complexity of the structure
  • Leverage
└ ─ ─ ─ ─ ─ ─ ─ ─ ─ ─ ─ ─ ─ ─ ─ ─ ─ ┘
```

• Regulatory design
• Tax
• Subsidy
• Payments to government

• Investment
• Quality of service
• Timing
• Other obligations

Tariff structure

Internal Rate of Return ?

Tariff level

Also
Type of restructuring:
• Degree/duration of exclusivity
• Composition of client base (poor/nonpoor)

Government
Firm
Regulator
Firm/regulator

Source: Authors.

all sources of cash flow fluctuations. They share responsibility in influencing the internal rate of return.

At the beginning of the process, the discount rate used to calculate the net present value of the cash flow is the weighted average cost of capital. The appropriate average tariff is the one that ensures a net present value of zero at that discount rate. Any change to the operational conditions of the operation or to the cost of capital will result in an imbalance between the internal rate of return and the cost of capital. If this change is structural, the scheduled and sometimes unscheduled tariff revisions will be designed to restore the equilibrium.

Conclusion

In the process of ordinary and extraordinary tariff revisions or contract renegotiations, the regulator always arbitrates between the interests of the various actors (users, operators, and government) that participate directly in the service to achieve certain goals using available regulatory instruments. The multiplicity of variables and interests simultaneously engaged in such processes requires that the processes

A2

be performed within an integral, consistent, and transparent analytical framework capable of quantifying the impact of regulatory decisions.

The integrity of the process implies that the regulator carry out the analysis using indicators that account for the economic, financial, and operating performance of the firm. For this purpose, the regulator needs to consider simultaneously all the variables affecting the economic equation, the minimum needs of finance, and the operator's operating conditions.

The transparency of a regulatory process is enhanced when all the relevant factors affecting the economic and financial variables of service provision are accounted for, and participants have access to such information.

The consistency of the analysis requires that all the variables affecting the indicators of the operator's performance are combined in a way that properly represents the behavior of market participants as well as sectoral, (quasi-)economic, and financial relations and constraints. Performance of this task will help ensure that implementation of regulatory instruments has a quantitative effect that reflects the actual situation of the concession under study.

To meet these criteria, the regulatory process may be performed through a regulatory model that combines the variables describing the service's initial condition, regulatory objectives, and regulatory instruments. The model allows the regulator to simulate new scenarios and test the sensitivity of the results to different assumptions in a more objective manner. Hence, regulatory decisions are less subjective and more robust for the uncertainties and risks that lie within and beyond the regulatory period.

The model can perform all the functions that any financial model of a firm would perform, but the model is designed with a longer-term view and explicitly identifies the key regulatory instruments. Thus, one of the elements to be taken into account by the regulator is that the firm can earn sufficient revenue to cover its costs (that is, operating costs, investments on fixed assets, and working capital) and to obtain a return equivalent to the opportunity cost of capital. For this purpose, the model forecasts the firm's net cash flow and internal rate of return, which the regulator compares with the cost of capital to determine the prices or revenues necessary to sustain service provision. Moreover, in the forecast financial statements, the model includes the key indicators for analyzing the firm's financial viability, which the regulator also considers in the regulatory process.

Although a regulatory model permits development of an appropriate regulatory process, it also poses at least two important challenges to regulators. The first is the necessity of using uniform quantifications of (quasi-)economic and financial benchmarks for, or indicators of, regulatory decisions. Then, the regulator is asked to focus on analysis of a group of variables, such as the cost of capital and the internal rate of return, as well as to fully understand the economic and financial concepts generating the trade-offs of various regulatory and policy instrument combinations in terms of their impacts on these indicators. The second challenge is that the quality of the model's results depends on the quality of the data used. Therefore, the regulator must generate a set of data—including quantification of the capital asset, service supply information, and demand and financial information—with a structure consistent with the model's requirements.

The analysis that can be performed with a regulatory model has certain limitations. The most important limitation arises from the use of spreadsheets, although new software programs have remarkably broadened the spectrum of the analysis that can be carried out with them.

A model is a way of representing the reality under analysis in a simplified manner. Therefore, the structure and degree of complexity of the model and the degree of disaggregation of the variables representing the real world will reflect judgments about what is critical (or not critical) for forecasting the future financial and economic outcomes. The success of the model will depend on the soundness of these judgments.

A2

Examples of Guidelines and Templates

This annex presents some guidelines and templates representative of the best practices in regulatory accounting.

Australia: Electricity Industry Guideline

Australia's Essential Services Commission (ESC) specifies requirements for "the collection, allocation and recording of business data by the licensee in the electricity supply in Victoria." Guideline 3 (ESC 2004a) establishes "a mechanism for the collection of information and certain recurring substantive information requirements" to enable the Commission

- to ensure the correct allocation of revenue and costs between the Distribution Business and non-distribution businesses;
- to inform **Electricity Distribution Price Determinations** and to perform other functions under relevant Acts;
- to measure actual financial performance of **Distribution Businesses** against forecast;
- to publish information on financial performance of Distribution Businesses;
- to improve the level(s) of transparency in the regulatory processes;
- to generally give effect to the objectives of the **Commission** as stated in the Essential Services Commission Act 2001 and the Electricity Industry Act 2000.

In addition, Guideline 3

- details the nature of information that the **Commission** will require to monitor the **Licensee's** performance;

- explains the way in which a **Licensee** must prepare separate accounts and maintain its accounting records;
- describes requirements for other information that a **Licensee** must report to the **Commission** to facilitate the **Commission's Electricity Distribution Price Determination**; and
- outlines a mechanism by which information that may be required by the **Commission** to fulfil its obligations and functions may be collected.

Australia: Regulatory Accounting Statements—Templates

The Australian Index to Regulatory Accounting Statements (ESC 2004b) includes

- Profit and Loss
- Balance Sheet
- Cash Flow
- Fixed Assets
  - Cost Opening
  - Cost Additions
  - Cost Disposals
  - Cost Closing
  - Additions by Reason
  - Additions by Reason (O'heads)
  - Depreciation Opening
  - Depreciation Annual Charge
  - Depreciation Disposals
  - Depreciation Closing
  - Written-down Value Opening
  - Written-down Value Movements
  - Written-down Value Disposals
  - Written-down Value Closing
- Maintenance by Asset Category
- Activity Areas
- Provision Accounts
- Noncausal Allocations
- Distribution Revenue
- Excluded Services and Other Activities
- Avoided Cost Payments

A3

Some of the templates specified in the index are presented.

Regulatory Accounting Statement   PL
Profit and Loss
For the period ended [   ]

Legal Entity Code/s	Statutory Account Code/s or Reference	Description	Audited Statutory Amount	Adjustments	Distribution Business	Excluded Services and Other Activities	Regulated by Price Cap
			$'000	$'000	$'000	$'000	$'000
		Distribution revenue			0		0
		Proceeds from sale of assets			0		0
		Customer contributions		0	0	xxxxx	xxxxx
		Other revenue			0		0
		Total Revenue	0	0	0	0	0
		Maintenance	0	0	0	0	0
		Grid fees	0	0	0	0	0
		Operating expenses	0	0	0	0	0
		Depreciation	0	0	0	0	0
		WDV assets disposed	0	0	0	0	0
		Other					
		Profit before Interest and Tax (PBIT	0	0	0	0	0
		Abnormals			0		0

In addition, it is mandatory to produce for each cost or revenue item that has been allocated to the Regulated Business Segments a supporting workpaper that includes the following:
(a) the amounts that have been directly attributed to each business segment
(b) the amounts that have been allocated to each business segment
(c) a description of the allocation basis
(d) the numeric quantity of each allocator.

A3

Regulatory Accounting Statement **BS**
Balance Sheet
As at [   ]

Legal Entity Code/s	Statutory Account Code or Reference	Description	Audited Statutory Amount	Adjustments	Distribution Business	Excluded Services and Other Activities	Regulated by Price Cap
			$'000	$'000	$'000	$'000	$'000
		CURRENT ASSETS					
		Cash			0		0
		Receivables			0		0
		Investments			0		0
		Prepayments			0		0
		Accrued revenue			0		0
		Inventories			0		0
		Other			0		0
		Total Current Assets	0	0	0	0	0
		NONCURRENT ASSETS					
		Receivables			0		0
		Investments			0		0
		Other			0		0
		Property, plant, and equipment	0	0	0	0	0
		Total Noncurrent Assets	0	0	0	0	0
		TOTAL ASSETS	0	0	0	0	0
		CURRENT LIABILITIES					
		Trade creditors and accruals			0		0
		Loans			0		0
		Customer deposits			0		0
		Bank overdraft			0		0
		Provisions			0		0
		Other			0		0
		Total current liabilities	0	0	0	0	0
		NONCURRENT LIABILITIES					
		Provisions			0		0
		Loans			0		0
		Other			0		0
		TOTAL LIABILITIES	0	0	0	0	0
		NET ASSETS /(LIABILITIES)	0	0	0	0	0

In addition, it is mandatory to produce for each asset or liability that has been allocated to the Regulatory Business Segments a supporting workpaper that includes the following
(a) the amounts that have been directly attributed to each business segment
(b) the amounts that have been allocated to each business segment
(c) a description of the allocation basis
(d) the numeric quantity of each allocator.

A3

Regulatory Accounting Statement
Cash Flow - Operations
For the period ended [ ]

CF

Legal Entity Code/s	Statutory Account Code or Reference	Description	Audited Statutory Amount	Adjustments	Distribution Business	Excluded Services and Other Activities	Regulated by Price Cap
		Receipts					
		Distribution revenue			0		0
		Proceeds from sale of assets			0		0
		Customer contributions			0		0
		Customer deposits			0		0
		Payments					
		Grid fees			0		0
		Operating expenses			0		0
		Movements in working capital			0		0
		Asset investment			0		0
		Customer refunds			0		0
		Net Operating Cash Flow	0	0	0	0	0

In addition, it is mandatory to produce for each cashflow item that has been allocated to the Regulated Business Segments a supporting workpaper that includes the following:

(a) the amounts that have been directly attributed to each business segment

(b) the amounts that have been allocated to each business segment

(c) a description of the allocation basis

(d) the numeric quantity of each allocator.

A3

Regulatory Accounting Statement
Fixed Assets at Cost - OPENING　　　　　　　　　　　　　　　　　　　　　　　　CO
Vesting Assets (V)　　　　　　　　　　　　　　　　　　　/　　/

Entity Code/s	Stat A/c Code	Statutory Accounts	Adjust.	Distrib. Business	Excluded/ Other	VOLTAGE			
						Subt'n	HV	LV	Other
		$'000	$'000	$'000	$'000	$'000	$'000	$'000	$'000
					0	xxxxx	xxxxx	xxxxx	xxxxx
				Subtransmission			xxxxx	xxxxx	xxxxx
				CBD		xxxxx			xxxxx
				Urban		xxxxx			xxxxx
				Rural – short		xxxxx			xxxxx
				Rural – long		xxxxx			xxxxx
				Nonstandard metering		xxxxx	xxxxx	xxxxx	
				Standard metering		xxxxx	xxxxx	xxxxx	
				Public lighting		xxxxx	xxxxx	xxxxx	
				SCADA/Network Control		xxxxx	xxxxx	xxxxx	
				Nonnetwork		xxxxx	xxxxx	xxxxx	
					0	0	0	0	0

Fixed Assets at Cost - OPENING
Post Vesting Assets (PV)

Entity Code/s	Stat A/c Code	Statutory Accounts	Adjust.	Distrib. Business	Excluded/ Other	VOLTAGE			
						Subt'n	HV	LV	Other
		$'000	$'000	$'000	$'000				
					0	xxxxx	xxxxx	xxxxx	xxxxx
				Subtransmission			xxxxx	xxxxx	xxxxx
				CBD		xxxxx			xxxxx
				Urban		xxxxx			xxxxx
				Rural – short		xxxxx			xxxxx
				Rural – long		xxxxx			xxxxx
				Nonstandard metering		xxxxx	xxxxx	xxxxx	
				Standard metering		xxxxx	xxxxx	xxxxx	
				Public lighting		xxxxx	xxxxx	xxxxx	
				SCADA/Network Control		xxxxx	xxxxx	xxxxx	
				Nonnetwork		xxxxx	xxxxx	xxxxx	
					0	0	0	0	0
				<– Customer contributions included in adjustments					

Total Pre & Post		0	0	0	0	0	0	0	0

A3

Regulatory Accounting Statement
Fixed Assets at Cost - ADDITIONS
Vesting Assets (V)

CA

/ /

Entity Code/s	Stat A/c Code	Statutory Accounts	Adjust.	Distrib. Business	Excluded/ Other	VOLTAGE			
						Subt'n	HV	LV	Other
		$'000	$'000	$'000	$'000				
		XXXXX	XXXXX	XXXXX	XXXXX	XXXXX	XXXXX	XXXXX	XXXXX
					Subtransmission	XXXXX	XXXXX	XXXXX	XXXXX
					CBD	XXXXX	XXXXX	XXXXX	XXXXX
					Urban	XXXXX	XXXXX	XXXXX	XXXXX
					Rural – short	XXXXX	XXXXX	XXXXX	XXXXX
					Rural – long	XXXXX	XXXXX	XXXXX	XXXXX
					Nonstandard metering	XXXXX	XXXXX	XXXXX	XXXXX
					Standard metering	XXXXX	XXXXX	XXXXX	XXXXX
					Public lighting	XXXXX	XXXXX	XXXXX	XXXXX
					SCADA/Network Control	XXXXX	XXXXX	XXXXX	XXXXX
					Nonnetwork	XXXXX	XXXXX	XXXXX	XXXXX

Fixed Assets at Cost - ADDITIONS
Post Vesting Assets (PV)

Entity Code/s	Stat A/c Code	Statutory Accounts	Adjust.	Distrib. Business	Excluded/ Other	VOLTAGE			
						Subt'n	HV	LV	Other
		$'000	$'000	$'000	$'000				
				0	0	XXXXX	XXXXX	XXXXX	XXXXX
					Subtransmission	0	XXXXX	XXXXX	XXXXX
					CBD	XXXXX	0	0	XXXXX
					Urban	XXXXX	0	0	XXXXX
					Rural – short	XXXXX	0	0	XXXXX
					Rural – long	XXXXX	0	0	XXXXX
					Nonstandard metering	XXXXX	XXXXX	XXXXX	0
					Standard metering	XXXXX	XXXXX	XXXXX	0
					Public lighting	XXXXX	XXXXX	XXXXX	0
					SCADA/Network Control	XXXXX	XXXXX	XXXXX	0
					Nonnetwork	XXXXX	XXXXX	XXXXX	0
				0		0	0	0	0
					<-- Customer contributions included in adjustments				

| Total Pre & Post | | 0 | 0 | 0 | 0 | 0 | 0 | 0 | 0 |

A3

Regulatory Accounting Statement
Fixed Assets Depreciation - OPENING   / /   DO
Vesting Assets (V)

Entity Code/s	Stat A/c Code	Statutory Accounts	Adjust.	Distrib. Business	Excluded/ Other	VOLTAGE			
						Subt'n	HV	LV	Other
		$'000	$'000	$'000	$'000				
				0		xxxxx	xxxxx	xxxxx	xxxxx
					Subtransmission		xxxxx	xxxxx	xxxxx
					CBD	xxxxx			xxxxx
					Urban	xxxxx			xxxxx
					Rural – short	xxxxx			xxxxx
					Rural – long	xxxxx			xxxxx
					Nonstandard metering	xxxxx	xxxxx	xxxxx	
					Standard metering	xxxxx	xxxxx	xxxxx	
					Public lighting	xxxxx	xxxxx	xxxxx	
					SCADA/Network Control	xxxxx	xxxxx	xxxxx	
					Nonnetwork	xxxxx	xxxxx	xxxxx	
				0		0	0	0	0

Fixed Assets Depreciation - OPENING
Post Vesting Assets (PV)

Entity Code/s	Stat A/c Code	Statutory Accounts	Adjust.	Distrib. Business	Excluded/ Other	VOLTAGE			
						Subt'n	HV	LV	Other
		$'000	$'000	$'000	$'000				
				0		xxxxx	xxxxx	xxxxx	xxxxx
					Subtransmission		xxxxx	xxxxx	xxxxx
					CBD	xxxxx			xxxxx
					Urban	xxxxx			xxxxx
					Rural – short	xxxxx			xxxxx
					Rural – long	xxxxx			xxxxx
					Nonstandard metering	xxxxx	xxxxx	xxxxx	
					Standard metering	xxxxx	xxxxx	xxxxx	
					Public lighting	xxxxx	xxxxx	xxxxx	
					SCADA/Network Control	xxxxx	xxxxx	xxxxx	
					Nonnetwork	xxxxx	xxxxx	xxxxx	
				0		0	0	0	0
				<– Customer contributions included in adjustments					

| Total Pre & Post | | 0 | 0 | 0 | 0 | 0 | 0 | 0 | 0 |

A3

Regulatory Accounting Statement   **AR**
Fixed Assets at Cost - ADDITIONS by REASON   /   /

(Net of Customer Contributions)		Regulated by Price Cap			
$'000	Total	VOLTAGE			
		Subt'n	HV	LV	Other
DEMAND RELATED					
Reinforcements					
Subtransmission			xxxxx	xxxxx	xxxxx
CBD		xxxxx			xxxxx
Urban		xxxxx			xxxxx
Rural – short		xxxxx			xxxxx
Rural – long		xxxxx			xxxxx
	0	0	0	0	0
New Customer Connections					
Subtransmission			xxxxx	xxxxx	xxxxx
CBD		xxxxx			xxxxx
Urban		xxxxx			xxxxx
Rural – short		xxxxx			xxxxx
Rural – long		xxxxx			xxxxx
	0	0	0	0	0
Load Movement					
Subtransmission			xxxxx	xxxxx	xxxxx
CBD		xxxxx			xxxxx
Urban		xxxxx			xxxxx
Rural – short		xxxxx			xxxxx
Rural – long		xxxxx			xxxxx
	0	0	0	0	0
NONDEMAND RELATED					
Reliability & Quality Maintained					
Subtransmission			xxxxx	xxxxx	xxxxx
CBD		xxxxx			xxxxx
Urban		xxxxx			xxxxx
Rural – short		xxxxx			xxxxx
Rural – long		xxxxx			xxxxx
	0	0	0	0	0
Reliability & Quality Improvements					
Subtransmission			xxxxx	xxxxx	xxxxx
CBD		xxxxx			xxxxx
Urban		xxxxx			xxxxx
Rural – short		xxxxx			xxxxx
Rural – long		xxxxx			xxxxx
	0	0	0	0	0
Environmental, Safety, & Legal					
Subtransmission			xxxxx	xxxxx	xxxxx
CBD		xxxxx			xxxxx
Urban		xxxxx			xxxxx
Rural – short		xxxxx			xxxxx
Rural – long		xxxxx			xxxxx
	0	0	0	0	0
TOTALS ACROSS VOLTAGE LEVELS					
Subtransmission		0	xxxxx	xxxxx	xxxxx
CBD		xxxxx	0	0	xxxxx
Urban		xxxxx	0	0	xxxxx
Rural – short		xxxxx	0	0	xxxxx
Rural – long		xxxxx	0	0	xxxxx
	0	0	0	0	0
Standard metering	0	xxxxx	xxxxx	xxxxx	
SCADA/Network Control	0	xxxxx	xxxxx	xxxxx	
Nonnetwork General - IT	0	xxxxx	xxxxx	xxxxx	
Nonnetwork General - Other	0	xxxxx	xxxxx	xxxxx	
RBPC - TOTAL ADDITIONS	0	0	0	0	0

		Excluded Services\Other			
$'000	Total				
Nonstandard metering	0	xxxxx	xxxxx	xxxxx	0
Public lighting	0	xxxxx	xxxxx	xxxxx	0
Other	0	xxxxx	xxxxx	xxxxx	0
Excl\Other - TOTAL ADDITIONS	0	0	0	0	0

TOTAL ALL ADDITIONS	0	0	0	0	0

A3

Regulatory Accounting Statement
Maintenance   MA
                                                                                                    /   /

Legal Entity Code/s	Statutory Account Code or Reference	$'000	Audited Statutory Amount	Adjustments	Distribution Business	Excluded Services and Other Activities	Regulated by Price Cap	VOLTAGE			
								Subt'n	HV	LV	Other
		Network									
		Subtransmission			0		0		XXXXX	XXXXX	XXXXX
		CBD			0		0	XXXXX			XXXXX
		Urban			0		0	XXXXX			XXXXX
		Rural – short			0		0	XXXXX			XXXXX
		Rural – long			0		0	XXXXX			XXXXX
		Nonstandard metering			0		XXXXX	XXXXX	XXXXX	XXXXX	
		Standard metering			0	XXXXX	0	XXXXX	XXXXX	XXXXX	
		Public lighting			0	0	XXXXX	XXXXX	XXXXX	XXXXX	
		SCADA/Network control			0		0	XXXXX	XXXXX	XXXXX	
		Other			0		0	XXXXX	XXXXX	XXXXX	
		Total	0	0	0	0	0	0	0	0	0

Regulatory Accounting Statement
Activity areas   AA

Legal Entity Code/s	Statutory Account Code or Reference	$'000	Audited Statutory Amount	Adjustments	Distribution Business	Excluded Services and Other Activities	Regulated by Price Cap
		Grid Fees					
		Transmission Connection Fee			0		0
		TUOS Charges			0		0
		Cross-Boundary Network Charges					
		Total	0	0	0	0	0
		Operating Costs					
					0		0
		Network operating costs			0		0
		Meter data services			0	0	XXXXX
		Billing & revenue collection			0		0
		Advertising/marketing			0		0
		Customer service			0		0
		Regulatory			0		0
		Goodwill amortization		0	XXXXX	XXXXX	XXXXX
		Other (See Apppendix 5)			0		0
		Total	0	0	0	0	0

Executive Remuneration (included above)	Audited Statutory Amount	Regulatory Adjustment	Allocated to Distribution Business	Excluded Services and Other Activities	Regulated by Price Cap
Amount in $'000s			0		0
Headcount			0		0
Average in $s	0	0	0	0	0

A3

Regulatory Accounting Statement
Provisions
A separate table is required for each provision

PA

Legal Entity Code/s	Statutory Account Code or Reference	<provision name>	Audited Statutory Amount	Adjustments	Distribution Business	Excluded Services and Other Activities	Regulated by Price Cap	Workpaper reference
		Opening Balance			0		0	
		Liabilities paid from provision			0		0	
		Increase in provision charged to profit			0		0	
		Other adjustments			0		0	
		Closing Balance	0	0	0	0	0	

In addition, it is mandatory to produce for each provision that has been allocated to the Regulated Business Segments a supporting
- written explanation of the need for the provision
- written explanation of the movements in the provision.

Workpaper supporting Regulatory Accounting Statements
Noncausal allocations
For the period ended [   ]

NA

No causal relationship could be established to allocate the items listed below. The amounts have been allocated to the regulated distribution business on the basis described which has been specifically approved by the office.

Description	Legal Entity Code/s	Statutory Account Code or Reference	Audited Statutory Amount	Adjustments (GL 3.4)	Distribution Business	Excluded Services and Other Activities	Regulated by Price Cap
			$'000	$'000	$'000	$'000	$'000
Basis of allocation:							

Reason for choosing this basis:

Date on which office approval granted:

A3

Regulatory Accounting Statement   DR
Distribution Revenue
For the period ended [   ]

Account Code	Distribution Category	Amount of Electricity Distributed	Distribution Revenue
			$'000
	Tariff categories		
	Total		

Regulatory Accounting Statement   AC
Avoided cost payments
For the period ended [   ]

Account Code		Avoided Cost Payment $	Number
	Deferral of augmentation to transmission networks		
	— Embedded generators		
	— Related party embedded generators		
	— Customers		
	— Other		
	Total		
	Deferral of augmentation to distribution networks		
	— Embedded generators		
	— Related party embedded generators		
	— Customers		
	— Other		
	Total		
	Metering cost deferral		
	— Embedded generators		
	— Related party embedded generators		
	— Customers		
	— Other		
	Total		
	Total		

A3

United Kingdom: Ofwat Regulatory Accounting Guideline

Ofwat's regulatory accounting guideline covers the requirements for accounting information, with three exceptions: the current cost accounting methodology, which is covered by regulatory accounting guideline 1 (RAG 1); the classification of expenditure (RAG 2); and the activity cost analysis and methodology (RAG 4).[1] The guideline addresses (1) the appointee's accounting statements, (2) the appointed business's activity cost analysis, (3) transactions with associated companies, and (4) audit and publication of accounting statements.

United Kingdom: Ofwat Regulatory Accounting Statements—Templates

According to Ofwat's regulatory accounting statements, all appointees must prepare a profit and loss account, a statement of assets and liabilities, and a statement of source and application of funds. Each of these statements must address the appointed business, the nonappointed business, and the total business of the appointee.

Regulatory accounting statements, "should, as far as is practicably possible, have the same content as the statutory annual accounts of the Appointee and be prepared in accordance with the formats and the accounting policies and principles which apply to those annual accounts" (Ofwat 2002a). Appointees are to use one format to present the information in the regulatory accounts for all companies.

The Ofwat Index to Regulatory Accounting Statements consists of the

- historic cost profit and loss account,
- historic cost balance sheet,
- historic cost balance sheet reconciliation to statutory accounts,
- current cost profit and loss account and current cost balance sheet,
- cash flow statement and analysis of turnover and operating income,
- current cost analysis of fixed assets by asset type and service,
- current cost working capital,
- movement on current cost reserve,
- reconciliation of current cost operating profit to net cash flow from operating activities,
- analysis of net debt,
- regulatory capital value, and
- five-year rolling summary—profit and loss, and five-year rolling summary—balance sheet disaggregated activities.

A3

Some of the templates specified in the index are presented.

Historic Cost Profit and Loss Account
for the Twelve Months
ended 31 March 20XX

	Note	Current Year			Prior Year		
		Appointed	Nonappointed	Total	Appointed	Nonappointed	Total
Turnover	(b)	I	I	C	I	I	C
Operating costs	(b)	I	I	C	I	I	C
Operating income	(b)	I	I	C	I	I	C
Operating profit	(b)	C	C	C	C	C	C
Other income	(b)	I	I	C	I	I	C
Interest receivable	(b)	I	I	C	I	I	C
Interest payable	(b)	I	I	C	I	I	C
Profit on ordinary activities Before taxation		C	C	C	C	C	C
Taxation – current	(b)	I	I	C	I	I	C
– deferred		I	I	C	I	I	C
Profit on ordinary activities After taxation		C	C	C	C	C	C
Extraordinary items	(b)	I	I	C	I	I	C
Profit for the year		C	C	C	C	C	C
Dividends	(b)	I	I	C	I	I	C
Retained profit for year		C	C	C	C	C	C

I: input

C: calculation

(a) Note required; see separate table for further analysis.

(b) Note required only if different from statutory accounts note.

A3

Historic Cost Balance Sheet
as of 31 March 20XX

	Note	Current Year			Prior Year		
		Appointed	Nonappointed	Total	Appointed	Nonappointed	Total
Fixed assets							
Tangible assets	(b)	I	I	C	I	I	C
Investment		I	I	C	I	I	C
Total fixed assets		C	C	C	C	C	C
Current assets							
Stocks		I	I	C	I	I	C
Debtors	(b)	I	I	C	I	I	C
Cash at bank and in hand		I	I	C	I	I	C
Short-term investments		I	I	C	I	I	C
Total current assets		C	C	C	C	C	C
Creditors: Amounts falling due within one year	(b)						
Borrowings		I		C	I	I	C
Dividends payable		I		C	I	I	C
Other creditors		I		C	I	I	C
Total creditors		C	C	C	C	C	C
Net current assets		C	C	C	C	C	C
Total assets less current liabilities		C	C	C	C	C	C
Creditors: Amounts falling due after one year	(b)						
Borrowing		I	I	C	I	I	C
Other creditors		I	I	C	I	I	C
Total creditors		I	I	C	I	I	C
Provisions for liabilities & charges	(b)						
- Deferred tax		I	I	C	I	I	C
- Other provisions		I	I	C	I	I	C
Deferred income	(b)	I	I	C	I	I	C
Net assets employed		C	C	C	C	C	C
Capital and reserves							
Called up share capital		I	I	C	I	I	C
Share premium		I	I	C	I	I	C
Profit & loss account		I	I	C	I	I	C
Other reserves	(b)	I	I	C	I	I	C
Capital & reserves		C	C	C	C	C	C

I: input

C: calculation

(a) Note required; see separate table for further analysis

(b) Note required only if different from statutory accounts note

A3

Current Cost Analysis of Fixed Assets by Asset Type				

Water Services

	Specialized Operational Assets	Nonspecialized Operational Properties	Infrastructure Assets	Other Tangible Assets	Total
Gross replacement cost					
At 1 April 20XX	I	I	I	I	C
AMP adjustment	I	I	I	I	C
RPI adjustment	I	I	I	I	C
Disposal	I	I	I	I	C
Additions	I	I	I	I	C
At 31 March 20XX	C	C	C	C	C
Depreciation					
At 1 April 20XX	I	I	I	I	C
AMP adjustment	I	I	I	I	C
RPI adjustment	I	I	I	I	C
Disposals	I	I	I	I	C
Charge for year	I	I	I	I	C
At 31 March 20XX	C	C	C	C	C
Net book amount at 31 March 20XX	C	C	C	C	C
Net book amount at 1 April 20XX	C	C	C	C	C

I: input
C: calculation

A3

**Current Cost Cash Flow
Statement for Twelve Months
Ended 31 March 20XX**

	Current Year			Prior Year		
	Appointed	Nonappointed	Total	Appointed	Nonappointed	Total
Net cash flow from operating activities	I	I	C	I	I	C
Returns on investments & servicing of finance						
Interest received	I	I	C	I	I	C
Interest paid	I	I	C	I	I	C
Interest in finance lease rentals	I	I	C	I	I	C
~~Preference~~ Non-equity dividends paid	I	I	C	I	I	C
Net cashflow from returns on investment & servicing of finance	C	C	C	C	C	C
Taxation						
~~UK corporation tax~~ paid	I	I	C	I	I	C
Capital expenditure and financial investment						
Gross cost of purchase of fixed assets	I	I	C	I	I	C
Receipt of grants and contributions	I	I	C	I	I	C
Infrastructure renewals expenditure	I	I	C	I	I	C
Disposal of fixed assets	I	I	C	I	I	C
Net cash outflow from investing activities						
Acquisitions and disposals	I	I	C	I	I	C
Equity dividends paid	I	I	C	I	I	C
Management of liquid resources						
Withdrawals from short-term deposits	I	I	C	I	I	C
Disposal or redemption of other liquid assets	I	I	C	I	I	C
Purchase of short-term deposits	I	I	C	I	I	C
Purchase of other liquid investments	I	I	C	I	I	C
Net cash flow from management of liquid resources	C	C	C	C	C	C
Net cash flow before financing	C	C	C	C	C	C
Financing						
Capital element in finance lease rentals	I	I	C	I	I	C
New bank loans	I	I	C	I	I	C
Repayment of bank loans						
Proceeds from share issues	I	I	C	I	I	C
Net cash inflow from financing	C	C	C	C	C	C
Increase (decrease) in cash and cash equivalents	C	C	C	C	C	C

I: input
C: calculation

A3

	Current Cost Working Capital	
	Current Year	**Prior Year**
Stocks	I	I
Trade debtors	I	I
Working cash balances	I	I
Trade creditors	I	I
Short-term capital creditors	I	I
Infrastructure renewals accrual/prepayment	I	I
Other accruals	I	I
Trade payments in advance	I	I
Payroll related taxes and social security contributions	I	I
Group trade debtors/(creditors)	I	I
Other short-term group debtors/(creditors)	I	I
Prepayments and other short-term debtors	I	I
Total working capital	C	C

I: input
C: calculation

A3

Analysis of Net Debt

	At 1 April 20XX	Cash Flow	Other Noncash Charges	Acquisitions	At 31 March 20XX
Cash in hand and bank	I	I	I	I	C
Overdrafts	I	I	I	I	C
Loans due after one year	I	I	I	I	C
Loans due within one year	I	I	I	I	C
Finance leases	I	I	I	I	C
Current asset investment	I	I	I	I	C
Total	C	C	C	C	C

I: input
C: calculation

Regulatory Capital Value

	Note	Current Year
Opening RCV for the year	(a)	I
Capital expenditure	(a)	I
Infrastructure renewals expenditure		I
Grants and contributions		I
Depreciation		I
Infrastructure renewals charge		I
Outperformance of Regulatory Assumptions (5 years in arrears)		I
Closing RCV carried forward	(a)	C
Average regulatory capital value		C

I: input
C: calculation

(a) Notes required : To explain that the table shows the RCV used in setting the price limits for the period 2000-01 to 2004-05; the differences from the actual capital expenditure and depreciation etc. will not affect price limits in the current period. Capital efficiencies will be taken into account in the calculation for the next periodic review.

Companies may also explain items which may be logged up and items of discretionary expenditure for possible inclusion in the RCV in future. The commentary should note that these items will require agreement with Ofwat prior to the next price-setting period.

A3

Published Activity Cost Table–Water and Sewerage Companies
Appointed Business–Revenue Account Only

£1000s	Service Analysis								Business Analysis		
	Water Supply			Sewerage Services							
	Resource & treatment	Distribution	Water supply subtotal	Sewerage	Sewage treatment	Sludge T&D Subtotal	Sewage T&D subtotal	Sewerage service subtotal	Customer services	Scientific services	Cost of regulaton
Direct Costs											
Employment Costs	I	I	C	I	I	I	C	C			
Power	I	I	C	I	I	I	C	C			
Agencies				I			C	C			
Hired and Cont. Services	I	I	C	I	I	I	C	C			
Associated Companies	I	I	C	I	I	I	C	C			
Materials and Consumables	I	I	C	I	I	I	C	C			
Service Charges	I	I	C	I	I	I	C	C			
Other Direct Costs		I	C	I	I	I	C	C			
Total Direct Costs	C	C	C	C	C	C	C	C	I	I	I
General & Support Exp.	I	I	C	I	I	I	C	C	I	I	I
Functional Expenditure	C	C	C	C	C	C	C	C	C	C	C
Capital Costs											
CC Depreciation	I	I	C	I	I	I	C	C			
Infrastructure Ren. Exp.	I	I	C	I	I		C	C			
Inf. Ren. Accrual/Prepayment	I	I	C	I			C	C			
Functional Cost	C	C	C	C	C	C	C	C			
Total (from above)			I					I			
Rates			I					I			
Doubtful Debts			I					I			
Exceptional			I					I			
Intangible Assets			I					I			
Business Acts. Cap. Costs			I					I			
Service Cost			C					C			
Services for Third Parties			I					I			
Total			C					C			
CCA (MEA) Values											
Service Activities	I	I	C	I	I	I	C	C			
Business Activities			I	I			I	C			
Service Totals			C	I			C	C			
Services for Third Parties			I					I			
Total			C					C			

I: Input
C: Calculation

Notes

1. The current RAGs and drafts for consultation are available at www.ofwat.gov.uk/aptrix/ofwat/publish.nsf/Content/navigation-publications-regulatoryaccountingguidelines.

A3

Impacts of Alternative Depreciation Profiles

Treatment of depreciation is an important issue for the regulator for several reasons. First, because regulated utilities are capital-intensive industries, depreciation is a major component of costs. Second, flexibility in the approach to calculating depreciation is considerable, resulting in a wide range of supportable profiles of depreciation charges over time. Used judiciously, these profiles can smooth prices and cash flows. But changes in depreciation profiles can also result in windfall gains and losses if not handled carefully. Third, depreciation profiles can help reduce risk for the investor. A greenfield gas pipeline may benefit from low or negative depreciation in its early years of operation, when it seeks to build the volume of gas transported. Conversely, a utility concerned about the threat of technological or policy change for the use of current assets (for example, electricity network or generation assets) may benefit from a higher depreciation rate in the early years to reduce future market or regulatory risks.

Perspectives on depreciation

For the accountant, depreciation is a means of allocating the outlays on physical long-term assets as expenses of earning revenue in measuring periodic income. Depreciation is central to the generally accepted accounting principle of matching costs to the revenues earned in each period.[1] Hence, the primary purpose of depreciation is to allocate the net cost of the asset over the asset's effective working life in a systematic and rational way. The starting point is the cost of acquiring the asset, and the end point is its residual value.

For the economist, depreciation is the change in the market value of the asset over a period (normally a year). In this sense, depreciation is a direct measure of economic income (being a change in net wealth). However, it does not matter whether the change in value is owing to obsolescence, wear and tear, or a change in exchange rates that affected the cost of a new equivalent asset. The accounting and economic perspectives share the same starting point (the cost of acquiring the asset) and end point (the asset's residual value). Thus, net depreciation over the life of the asset is the same.

In neither perspective is depreciation a means of funding the replacement of assets, although it is often viewed that way. Depreciation is a noncash expense, and when regulated prices are set at the sum of costs including depreciation, higher depreciation will provide increased cash flows during that period.[2] However, these higher cash flows will be offset by lower depreciation and lower cash flows in other periods.

Straight-line depreciation is the most common means of determining accounting depreciation, but many other methods, such as reducing balance or production unit depreciation (see discussion below), are possible. The economists' view of depreciation is arguably more precise in theory but less useful in practice for the regulator. For most of the assets commonly owned by a regulated operator, there exists no second-hand market that is independent of the prices set by the regulator for the services provided. Attempts to calculate economic depreciation require an assumption of the prices that the regulator is to set. Hence, an element of circularity arises.[3]

Regulatory approaches to depreciation

The regulator will need to consider the full range of regulatory objectives in setting depreciation requirements. Economic objectives will be important, but which of the most commonly used approaches may most nearly approach economic depreciation remains unclear. In practice, the pattern of economic depreciation—the change in the market value of an asset—is likely to differ between different asset classes (for example, buildings and motor vehicles) even within a single utility. Therefore, flexibility in depreciation profiles is considerable, and the choice of profiles may reflect other objectives that can provide clearer guidance, such as administrative simplicity, certainty and consistency, price stability, and intergenerational equity.

Depreciation profiles can affect the risks to asset owners of asset underutilization or obsolescence. When these risks are beyond the operator's control, there can be merit in using depreciation profiles to reduce these risks through, say, accelerated depreciation. However, the operator can often manage these risks to some

A4

extent. It may be able to defer or stage capital expenditure to reduce its postexpenditure risks and reduce the risk of low capacity utilization through alternative pricing structures. Hence, using depreciation to minimize postexpenditure risk is not necessarily optimal.

In determining the approach to regulation, the key requirements for the regulator are likely to be the following:

- The total (accumulated) depreciation over the asset's life is equal to the difference between the undepreciated value and the residual value of the asset.
- Following from the previous point, any changes to the depreciation profile have a net present value–neutral effect on prices and the income stream.
- The approach is transparent, administratively simple, and consistent with intergenerational equity.

Alternative approaches to depreciation

Many depreciation methodologies, varying in complexity and profile of depreciation charges and prices over time, are available to the regulator.

Straight-line depreciation involves deduction of a constant percentage of the undepreciated asset value from the opening asset value in each year. In historic cost accounting, the result equates to a constant dollar amount found by dividing the initial cost of the asset by its expected life. Straight-line depreciation can be criticized as too simple and not properly reflecting declines in the service potential or market value of assets, but such depreciation is commonly used and easily applied.

Declining balance depreciation front-end loads depreciation (the dollar amount of depreciation is largest in the early years of asset life). Such depreciation is calculated as a constant proportion of the opening asset value for each period. It may be argued that this approach better reflects the pattern of change in the market value of some assets, such as motor vehicles. But arguably it does not reflect well the change in the market value of other assets, such as buildings.

Production unit depreciation involves estimation of the asset's total output and calculation of depreciation for each year on the basis of the actual year's output. This strategy may front-end load depreciation if use of an asset, like electricity generators, is likely to decline over the asset's life. For other assets, such as substations, production unit depreciation may defer depreciation, because loadings on those assets may increase over their life. The production unit approach may be most useful for assets with gradually used capacity, such as pipelines or transmission assets,

A4

because it avoids excessive unit prices in the early years, when the assets may be lightly loaded.

Annuity depreciation is akin to the principal being repaid on a mortgage. For a given constant annual revenue the net present value of which is equal to the original cost of the asset, the depreciation in each period is the amount left after the deduction of a normal return on the opening value of the asset for the period. Annuity depreciation is not often used in business but is sometimes proposed for regulated utilities, because it yields a constant price over the asset's life and reduces potential price shocks as assets are replaced.

Estimation of asset lives

In principle, an asset should be depreciated over its expected productive life. This practice is not essential, but an artificially short asset life is likely to magnify volatility in prices over time and result in intergenerational inequities as current customers pay for resources to be used by future customers. Conversely, asset lives that are too long may raise funding concerns and result in intergenerational inequities as future customers pay for resources used by current customers.

One challenge is to estimate asset lives accurately. The condition, and even the age, of current assets may not be well known. The long life of infrastructure assets also means that their useful economic lives may be difficult to estimate. The uncertainties of obsolescence through technological change (for example, new, more economic generation technologies) or policy change (for example, limits on outputs due to environmental concerns) make it difficult to estimate asset lives 30–50 years into the future. Some assets (such as water mains or aging gas pipelines) may not be replaced but may have their service lives continually extended through maintenance and new technologies. In these cases, a renewal accounting approach may be appropriate. Estimating total production over the asset's life under a production unit approach may be even more difficult than estimating the asset's life in years.

Changing the assumed age of assets from time to time may be warranted. Changing this age should be done carefully and prospectively. There should be no modification of past depreciation or re-estimation of the opening asset value on the basis of the new assumed asset lives. The reasons are illustrated by (1) the impact of different approaches to calculating depreciation on the recovering profile of depreciation expenses and prices and revenues over time, and (2) the effect of changing the approach to calculating depreciation or changing the assumed asset life midway through an asset's life. The examples below simplify analysis of

A4

this impact and this effect by assuming one asset rather than numerous assets of different ages and by assuming that regulated prices and revenues are established from the build-up of costs (including a return on the asset base) so that the depreciation profile is directly related to the price and revenue profile.

Impact of different approaches to calculating depreciation

Figures A4.1 and A4.2 compare straight-line, annuity, and declining balance depreciation and the resulting price profiles. All values are in constant prices. Assumptions are as follows: (1) the asset costs 100 units and has a 40-year economic life; (2) to derive the annuity depreciation, the weighted average cost of capital is 7 percent (real); (3) for the diminishing balance depreciation the first year is double that of straight-line depreciation (that is, double declining balance), but a switch is made to straight-line depreciation after year 20.

Each depreciation profile yields income streams with the same net present value over the life of the assets, but the depreciation in any given year can vary significantly among the depreciation profiles. In practice, however, the extreme differences

Figure A4.1 Depreciation Charge Profiles over Time

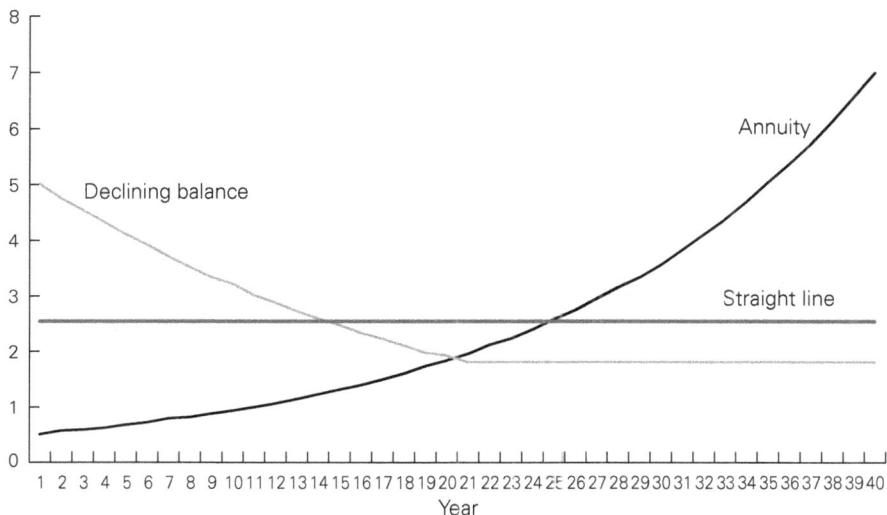

Source: Allen Consulting Group 2003, 20.

Figure A4.2 Prices over Time under Different Depreciation Charge Profiles

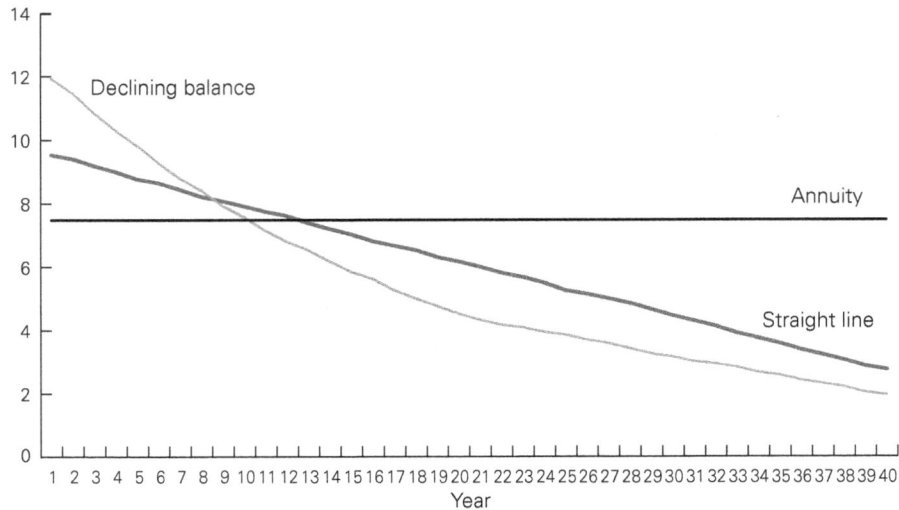

Source: Allen Consulting Group 2003, 21.

between the total depreciation charges in any year under the alternative profiles will not be observed, because an operator will have many assets of many different ages. Total depreciation will be the sum of the depreciation charge for individual assets of different ages; therefore, the effect of different depreciation profiles will be averaged out.

However, changing from one depreciation profile to another during an asset's life can create significant changes in prices and, if not handled carefully, windfall gains or losses.

Impact of changing depreciation profiles

Figures A4.3 and A4.4 show the impact of switching from straight-line depreciation to annuity depreciation after 15 years. Until year 15, the asset is depreciated on a straight-line basis. The depreciated value at the end of year 14 is then depreciated over the remaining 25 years on a declining balance basis. A consequence of changing depreciation profiles is that the change in depreciation and revenues may be significant. Depreciation drops below what it would have been if the declining balance were used from the start of the asset's life, and revenues also

A4

Figure A4.3 Switch from Straight-Line to Annuity Depreciation: Depreciation Profile

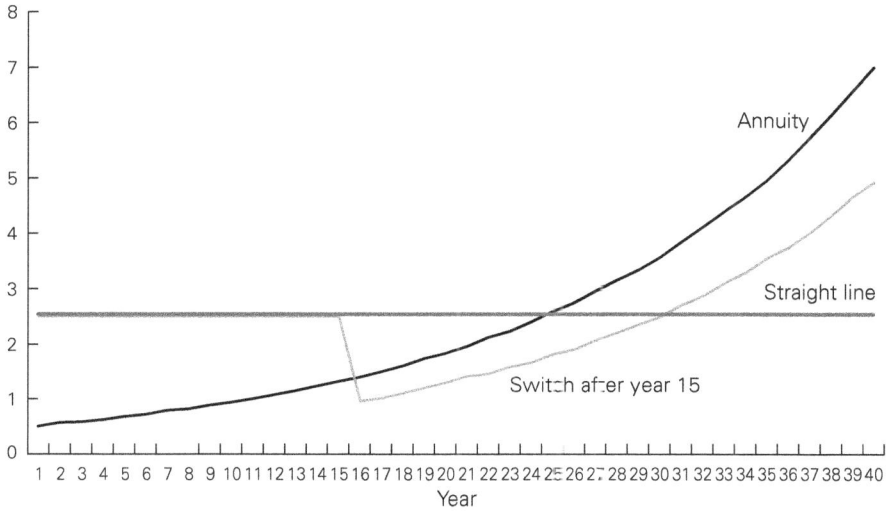

Source: Allen Consult ng Group 2003, 22.

Figure A4.4 Switch from Straight-Line to Annuity Depreciation: Price Effects

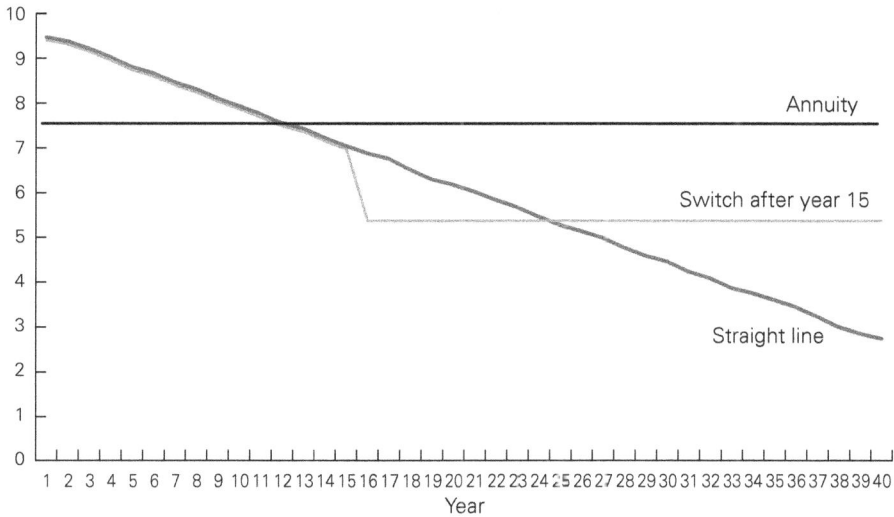

Source: Allen Consult ng Group 2003, 23.

drop sharply. However, because the depreciated value of the asset at the end of year 14 is used as the starting point, two highly desirable properties are preserved: total depreciation (undiscounted) over the asset's life is unchanged, and the income net present value of the net income stream over the asset's life is unchanged.

Under some systems, assets are revalued to their depreciated replacement cost at the start of the regulatory period. Depreciation would be double counted, to a degree, under these systems, and the new depreciation rate would be used to establish the opening asset value. In figures A4.3 and A4.4, annual depreciation and revenues track annuity lines as if the asset had been depreciated on an annuity basis from the outset. The result is that total depreciation over the asset's life exceeds the asset's original value and that the net present value of the income stream increases over the asset's life.

Impact of changing the assumed asset life

Changing an asset's assumed life midway through its life can have a similar effect (figure A4.5). In this example, optimized replacement costs are used to value the asset at the start of each regulatory period. Better asset maintenance, better assets, or better information may mean that assets are expected to have a longer service life. However, if the new asset life assumption is used to calculate the depreciated asset value, the asset is being double depreciated, resulting in a windfall gain for the operator. To avoid this result, the opening depreciated asset value has to be calculated under the previous asset life assumptions so that the change in assumed asset lives has only a prospective impact. If more than one change has been made in assumed asset lives, the opening asset value would need to be calculated sequentially using the relevant asset valuation assumption for each period.

Treatment of depreciation on variations from forecast capital expenditure

The issue of depreciation of the over- and underexpenditure relative to forecast may arise if a prospective price cap is set on the basis of forecast capital expenditure. Treatment of such depreciation will be linked to the regulator's approach to efficiency incentives.

One option is to roll forward the asset base between reviews by adding capital expenditure to the asset as incurred and depreciating the asset from that point using

A4

Figure A4.5 Revaluation of a Partially Depreciated Asset and a Fully Depreciated Asset

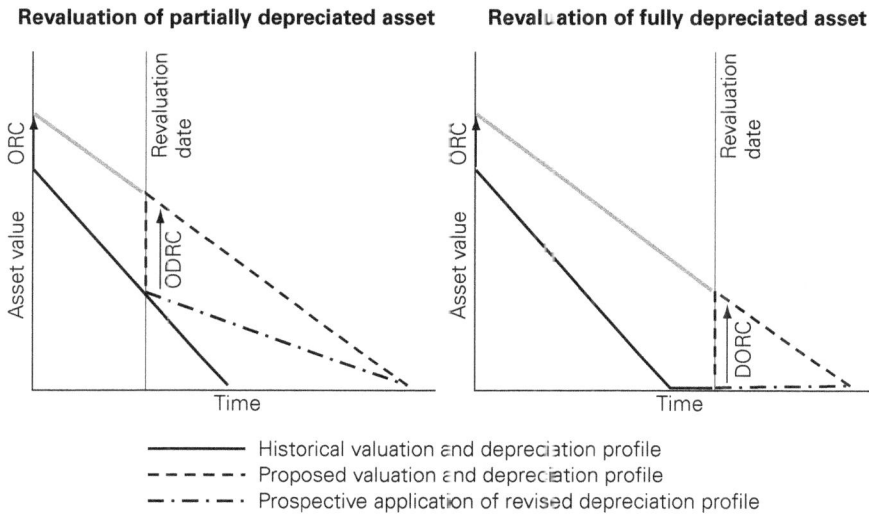

Revaluation of partially depreciated asset   Revaluation of fully depreciated asset

Legend:
——————— Historical valuation and depreciation profile
— — — — — Proposed valuation and depreciation profile
— · — · — · Prospective application of revised depreciation profile

Source: Authors.
ORC = Optimized replacement cost.
DORC = Depreciated optimized replacement cost.

the standard depreciation life for the asset. In this case, if expenditure is less than forecast, actual depreciation is less than that built into revenue and price controls. The converse applies to overexpenditures. Hence, incentives for greater efficiency are increased, but the risks for poor returns on unexpected capital expenditure requirements are also increased.

The other option is to roll forward the asset base by adding actual capital expenditure to the asset base and deducting the forecast depreciation. In effect, expenditure in excess of forecast expenditure is included in the next regulatory asset base at its undepreciated value—its depreciation is deferred, not forgone. The converse applies to underexpenditure. This treatment for over- and underexpenditures reduces incentives for efficiency improvements, but it also reduces risks for the operator from unexpected variations in capital expenditure requirements.

The regulator's primary obligation is to clearly specify the proposed treatment of depreciation in the roll forward of the asset base at the start of the regulatory period, and to incorporate this treatment in the accounting rules.

A4

Data requirements

Regulatory depreciation can be calculated at the various levels of disaggregation.

In principle, depreciation could be calculated at a highly aggregated level. Typically, a regulated operator will have a mix of system assets and nonsystem assets; variation between the two groups is often substantial. The balance between these categories of assets is likely to vary over time. Furthermore, if there are related-party transactions or unregulated outputs, the underlying activities are unlikely to use system assets and nonsystem assets in the same proportion as the core monopoly activities. For both reasons—variation in the composition of assets over time and variation between the related-party or unregulated activities and the monopoly activities—a split between system assets and nonsystem assets is likely to be the minimum requirement.

In practice, these reasons, together with the possible concern over allocation of costs among regulated service categories, are likely to result in the need for a more disaggregated approach. The challenge for the regulator is to balance the complexity of its financial modeling and the additional data burdens on the utility against the benefits of more accurate modeling of depreciation and attribution of costs.

Given the selected level of disaggregation, the regulator can specify the classification scheme for a regulatory asset register. This scheme is the basis for tracking depreciation, capital expenditure, disposals, and the roll forward of the regulatory asset base. The regulator will also need to specify the average asset life to be used for each asset category.

Principles for depreciation

Seven principles should guide regulatory treatment of depreciation:

- A simple, easily implemented approach to calculating depreciation, such as straight depreciation, is often preferred. However, some flexibility should be provided on this approach.
- The simplest, most easily implemented approach is unlikely to match economic depreciation, but whether economic depreciation would be front-end or back-end loaded depends on the operator's specific assets. No one approach is necessarily more likely to reflect the economic depreciation of individual assets than another.

A4

- Matching of regulatory depreciation with tax depreciation is neither likely nor necessarily desirable.
- Applying a uniform approach (but not uniform asset life) to all assets has strong merits, including clarity, simplicity, and easy verification.
- Maintaining a consistent approach to and assumptions about depreciation over time can help operators avoid uncertainty and the risks of windfall gains or losses.
- However, regulators should leave open the option of revising the depreciation profile and assumed asset lives in light of
  - changing information on assets' conditions and lives,
  - the need to avoid unnecessary exposure to potential market risks, and
  - the need to manage potential price or cash flow shocks.
- When assumed asset lives or depreciation profiles are changed, they should have a prospective impact—the opening asset value before the change should be estimated on the basis of the previous depreciation assumptions.

Notes

1. The matching principle requires "that the value of all resources consumed in the process of earning the current period's revenue must be charged against that revenue before any operating profit is earned" (Barton 1977, 74).

2. Although unregulated businesses may also be tempted to view depreciation as a source of cash flows, if prices are set in the market, net cash flow is the difference between cash revenues and cash expenses. Depreciation may account for a significant component of this gap. Changing the rate of depreciation provides no additional cash, but it does alter the allocation of free cash flows between profits and depreciation.

3. One suggestion is that the regulator should assume a uniform price for the asset's services over the asset's life and calculate the value of the asset at the end of each year on the basis of the net present value of the hypothetical income stream over the remainder of the asset's life. The resulting profile for depreciation is similar to the repayment of principal on a loan—low in the early years and high in the last years of the asset's life.

A4

List of Sample Performance Indicators

Technical performance indicators are quantitative or qualitative indicators related to a particular performance aspect of a company. These indicators can be related to values used as benchmarks to help explain positive or negative deviations from performance values. The final step in analysis of historical data is to put company performance in the context of overall industry performance and the performance of other similar companies in the region. Ratio analysis is then a valuable tool to assist the analyst in answering questions about how well the company is doing or how efficient it is compared with other companies.

However, any indicator portrays an incomplete picture of a company, because it often excludes other contributing factors (institutional, incentives). As a result, indicators cannot be used mechanically, and critical judgment is needed to interpret them.

Indicators are based on data from management information systems. Hence, having a reliable information system is as important as choosing the right indicators.

The following definitions (drawn from World Bank 1996) are some commonly used indicators:

- *Working ratio:* The working ratio is the ratio of operating costs to operating revenues. The common definition of this ratio excludes depreciation and interest payments from costs. When used for utilities analysis, sound financial management requires a working ratio well below 1. Caution should be used in interpreting this ratio when there is evidence that utilities are cutting down on maintenance costs that would improve the working ratio but that could lead to a critical situation in the future. The *operating ratio* is similar to the working ratio but includes depreciation and interest payments.

- *Personnel costs/operating costs:* Personnel costs are expressed as a ratio of total operating costs (depreciation and debt service excluded). Depreciation and debt are excluded because of the lack of uniformity in treating revaluation of fixed assets and to facilitate comparison of utilities with and without debt service obligations.
- *Staff productivity index:* This index relates the number of staff to the number of connections. As a guideline, a staff productivity index of less than 4 could be considered adequate, but with room for improvement. A reduction in the index cannot necessarily be interpreted as an increase in efficiency. To complete the analysis of staff productivity, expenditures on personnel (personnel costs/operating costs) also need to be examined. An alternative is an analysis based on production: number of staff/production (kilowatt hours for electricity or cubic meters for water, for example).
- *Unit operational cost:* This ratio is normally computed as operational costs/production. Differences in this ratio between companies can be associated with differences in quality levels.

There are also some technical indicators that regulators normally watch when dealing with quality issues, metering, and network length, among others:

- *Consumption:* Consumption is average daily consumption per person served or average daily consumption per connection served (for example, liters for water or kilowatt hours for electricity per capita per day). The distinction between user and connection is particularly important in countries where no individual metering exists, and different users are connected to one connection.
- *Network length:* This length is the length of distribution network as a function of number of people served (kilometers/users) or as a function of connections (kilometers/connections).
- *Distribution losses:* A major concern about utility operations is the level of losses. Basically, losses reflect the difference between deliveries to the distribution system and quantities sold. The level of losses is a good proxy for overall efficiency of operations. Distributional losses as defined here include physical losses as well as commercial losses (illegal connections). Other definitions can isolate the effect of commercial losses. The two types of losses have different regulatory implications: physical losses can be reduced to a certain minimum (and hence there is an optimal allowed level of optimal losses), but commercial losses can be reduced by a company's specific actions against illegal connections.

Cost Allocation: Illustration of a Step-by-Step Approach

Consider a simple case in which a company produces two products, A and B, and management wants to undertake a detailed cost analysis of each product. Management already has the information about the revenues generated by A and B separately, because this information is usually easy to obtain.

Step 1: Identify cost objectives

Identify the cost objectives—in this case, product A and product B.

Step 2: Identify direct costs

On the basis of accounting information and knowledge of costs and production process, identify direct costs.

First, identify all direct costs—all costs that can easily be traced directly to product A or product B, such as direct labor costs (salary costs of workers involved only in the production of product A or product B) and direct materials (raw materials used only in the production of product A or product B). Figure A6.1 illustrates the process.

Step 3: Classify indirect costs and allocate cost pools to cost objectives

Classify all remaining costs, which are indirect costs, into categories related to each of the cost objectives, and group them into cost pools. On the basis of activity-based costing, identify all the different activities involved in the production of

Figure A6.1 Identifying Direct Costs

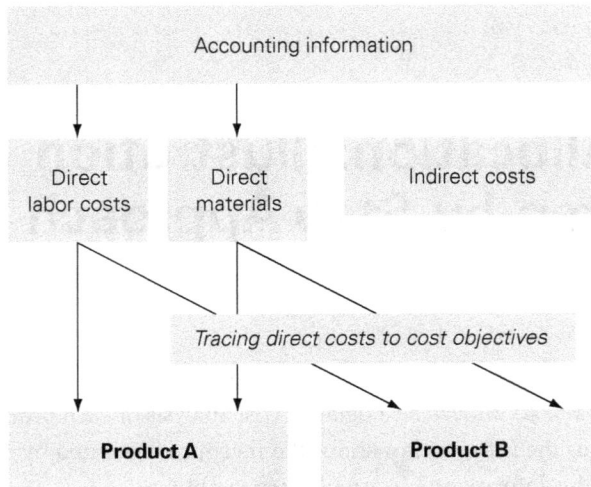

product A and product B, such as purchasing, customer management, and so on. Then identify the cost allocation bases to allocate the different cost pools to the cost objectives (figure A6.2).

Figure A6.2 Classifying Indirect Costs and Allocating Cost Pools to Cost Objectives

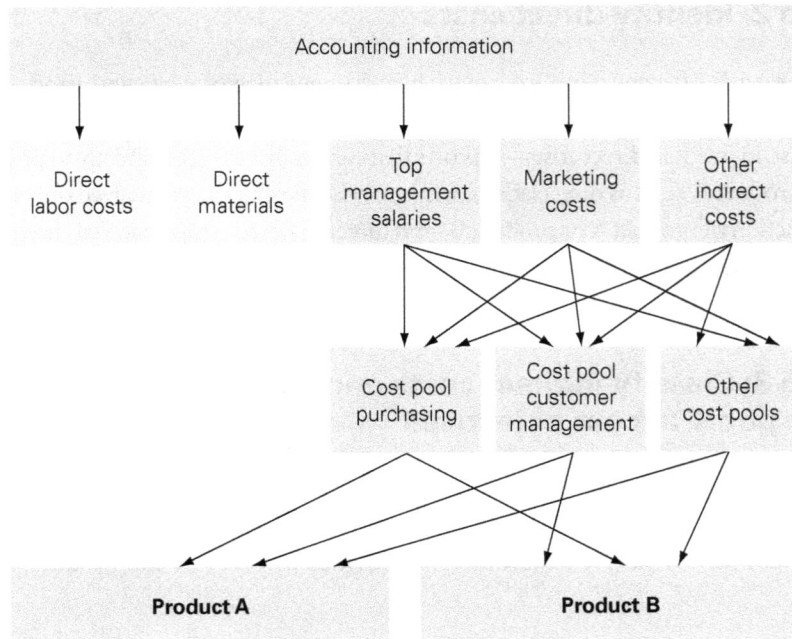

A6

Box A6.1 provides an example of this process for power and maintenance costs.

Box A6.1 Example of Allocation of a Specific Pool of Costs: Power and Maintenance Costs (overhead manufacturing costs)

Different machines are necessary to produce products A and B. The direct costs (direct labor and direct raw materials) linked to the machines have been traced easily to each product. Now other indirect costs have to be allocated. All costs linked to use of machines, such as power and maintenance, could be regrouped. *Machine hours* can be chosen as the cost driver that explains the variations of power cost and maintenance cost (the more machine hours, the higher the power and maintenance costs). After all costs related to power and maintenance are regrouped in a specific cost pool, the costs for that pool are totaled. Then the total cost of that pool is divided by the number of machine hours to obtain the pool rate, which equals cost / machine hour. Then the number of machine hours used to produce product A is estimated, and the cost (number of machine hours multiplied by pool rate) of product A is assigned.

Source: Authors.

A6

Regulatory Asset Base Valuation

The overview of international experience presented below suggests that consensus on the best way to value the assets of a regulated firm does not exist. Regardless of the method adopted, a basic requirement is consistency in the valuation of assets over time.

The U.S. Interstate Commerce Commission (ICC) considered replacement cost based on present values to be "impractical, extremely expensive and subjected to great differences of opinion regarding the value," and other regulatory agencies concluded that "the net effect of this load is that the commission's ability to properly serve users is endangered" (Goodman 1998, 770). Another drawback of replacement cost is the underlying assumption that the existing plant would be exactly reproduced, an unlikely occurrence if the plant had to be rebuilt at current prices and in light of the possibility that a more efficient or economic plant might be built.

In the case of recently privatized companies, the use of replacement cost for valuing assets results in efficient tariffs from an allocative point of view; however, it gives investors an extraordinary return on capital against users every time the concession fee is lower than said replacement cost.

In view of all these problems, U.S. regulatory practice finally settled on use of the original (historic) cost of assets (Goodman 1998, 775, 777), which is represented by the cash spent on the property engaged in the public service, and regulators resorted to the company's books to get the relevant information for the asset base valuation. An advantage of this method, as reported in Goodman (1998, 776), is that "it is based on well defined facts; it is not subject to unlimited imagination or sharp fluctuations of prices and, therefore, it represents a more accurate measure of the value on which the owner will be allowed to earn a return—through tariffs [...]." At the same time, it "stabilizes tariffs so economic shocks are greatly reduced...." (Goodman 1998, 776). According to Goodman (1998, 776–77),

the arguments in favor of using the original cost to calculate the asset base are overwhelming....it is quite simple and objective to determine the original cost... the use of a fair value rather than the original cost calls for substantially more preparation on the company and agency's staff, whose costs are ultimately supported by the consumers.

Privatization of public utilities introduces a new dimension to this valuation problem, because the sale in itself implies, to some extent, breaking with the previous situation. This dimension came to regulators' attention with privatizations in the United Kingdom. The market value of electricity, gas, and water companies at the time of privatizations was substantially lower than the historic cost (adjusted) of the companies' assets. Applying the cost of capital to said cost resulted in a return for the company that appeared to be unfairly split between shareholders and consumers.

The Monopolies and Mergers Commission (MMC) initially resolved this matter in its review of British Gas (MMC 1993). The commission decided to compensate investors on the basis of the market value of their assets on a specific postprivatization date, rather than on the basis of replacement cost. This approach has become common practice for determination of the regulatory value of assets (Grout 1997).

Slightly different variants of this approach are also in use. For example, asset value can be determined on the basis of market value on a specific date; in this case, the cost of capital employed for the old assets (before that date) is not the total cost of capital but that amount reduced by the market-to-asset ratio. The UK general director of electricity based his proposals for regulatory value of assets on the initial market value of the company (at the end of the first day of operations). He argued that the expectations revealed by investors was a more solid basis on which to determine the company's value than the book value of assets or the value set by the government for the privatization (flotation price) (MMC 1997). In his opinion, investor expectations would take into account any deliberate undervaluation of shares made to ensure the success of the sale. The director general believed that investors had to be compensated for what they had actually paid.

During its review of electricity distribution companies, the UK Office of Electricity Regulation (OFFER) stated that

A7

it is appropriate to take into account the money effectively paid to purchase the company, and not just the accounting value of assets. The valuation of a company at the moment of "flotation" reflects what the original shareholders considered to be the prospective flow of future dividends, taking into account the information in a very detailed Prospect and the risks associated to the investment and valuing each company completely. It would be wrong not to consider this matter fairly important. (OFFER 1994)

On the other hand, using the amount actually paid by investors at the moment of privatization can be disadvantageous, because it may result in inefficient tariffs from the standpoint of allocative efficiency (because the tariffs fall below the economic cost of service provision), though fair from the point of view of effective capital investment. The main objection to use of this method is the circular nature of the determination: what the company paid during privatization represents the net present value of future cash flow, and the cash flow depends on tariffs set in the future. This method would, in theory, remove any limit on the amount to be paid by the company. If the principle were applied, the next tariff review would necessarily incorporate the purchase value into tariffs, thus ensuring a fair and reasonable rate of return on whatever was paid for the assets. This circularity problem between market value and tariffs is not relevant during tariff review, because the idea that the amount to be paid by the company is unlimited is completely untrue. The circularity argument can be strictly applied only to determination of tariffs and the value of capital at the same moment in time.

As regards privatizations, OFFER sets tariffs, on the basis of which it determines a company's value. At the tariff review, the value of capital is given by the price paid at the privatization so that the value can be used to determine tariffs without raising circularity problems.

In other countries, particularly in Chile, regulation is based almost exclusively on the replacement value of a system economically adapted to expected level of demand in a predefined time horizon (typically five years). This so-called model efficient company method rests on the idea of promoting efficient tariffs from the point of view of allocation, without considering sustainability to any great extent.

In regulation of the model efficient company in Chile, valuation departs from the depreciated optimized replacement cost (DORC), because for each tariff review, 100 percent of the assets necessary to meet demand are considered but are unadjusted according to their economic life. In this sense, the regulated asset base has no relation to the investment effectively carried out by the company.

A7

In Australia, the statement of principles for the regulation of electricity network revenues establishes the framework for a sector's regulation. The statement proposes that the maximum value for the regulatory asset base be given by the DORC of a transmission company's assets. The DORC valuation of the regulatory asset base is rolled forward between reviews by adding proposed capital expenditure and deducting depreciation. At the next review, a new estimate of the DORC may be made.

Determination of a DORC valuation involves three stages. First, the optimal configuration (network setup) of assets is identified. Second, the costs of the assets that would form part of this optimal network are calculated. Finally, the assets are depreciated using the standard economic life of the asset, together with an estimate of the asset's remaining life.

Valuation approach

To establish required revenue, the regulator must first clarify what constitutes the opening asset base. The approach to be adopted for valuing the opening asset base and the revenue necessary to cover an appropriate rate of return on assets will be influenced by interpretation of the asset base's nature.

The point is to determine whether the asset base represents shareholders' financial investments in the firm (maintenance of the firm's financial capital in real terms) or the firm's physical assets (the company's ability to keep the same output level of assets over time). Box A7.1 summarizes the two alternatives, as defined by the Accounting Standards Committee for the United Kingdom.

The amount taken as the return on capital will depend on the approach, whether based on physical assets or financial investments. If the financial investments approach is adopted, the amount will represent the profit needed to maintain the purchasing power of the investments made by shareholders. If the physical capital approach is adopted, the return on capital will be represented by the amount of depreciation of the sum required to replace (or renew) the stock of existing assets, when and as needed. In some cases, both approaches can be equivalent, though significantly different.

It could be argued that, under the physical capital approach, assets paid for or contributed by consumers augment a company's capacity to provide services and therefore should be included in the calculation. Furthermore, these assets will eventually be replaced or renovated. A financial view of the asset base would exclude

---

**Box A7.1 Two Valuation Approaches Defined
by the UK Accounting Standards Committee**

The UK Accounting Standards Committee handbook, *Accounting for the Effects of Changing Prices* (1986), discusses two alternative measures of a company's profits.

Real *financial capital maintenance* is concerned with maintenance of the real financial capital of a company and with the company's ability to continue financing its functions. Under real financial capital maintenance, profit is measured after provision has been made to maintain the purchasing power of opening financial capital. This calculation involves use of a general inflation index such as the retail price index. Real financial capital maintenance, therefore, addresses the principal concerns of shareholders. In the absence of general inflation, real financial capital maintenance is equivalent to conventional historical cost accounting, with the exception of the treatment of unrealized holding gains.

Operating capability maintenance is concerned with maintenance of the physical output capability of a company's assets. Profit is measured after provision has been made for replacing the output capability of a company's physical assets (a major concern of management). This operation involves use of specific inflation indexes, such as the construction price index or the Baxter index, to adjust asset values. This approach was used in Statement of Standard Accounting Practice (SSAP) 16—Current Cost Accounting (this standard was withdrawn).

Source: Authors.

A7

---

assets paid for or contributed by consumers from calculation of assets in determination of required revenue, because these assets are not part of the financial capital invested by shareholders. It could be argued that their inclusion would result in the user paying twice for the same asset.

The asset base used to determine the return will vary, depending on the concepts chosen. From the financial investment perspective, the monetary investment should be adjusted if the purchasing power of the currency changes. Under the physical capital approach, the asset base will vary according to asset replacement expense.

Table A7.1 Advantages and Disadvantages of Financial Investment and Physical Capital Approaches

	Financial investment approach	Physical capital approach
Advantages	• It is simple. There is no need to value the replacement costs of specific assets or make adjustments for obsolescence. • It ensures maintenance of the purchasing power of the opening investment, which represents the main requirement from the investor's point of view.	• It focuses on maintaining the firm's output capacity—the services rendered to customers. • It allows adjustments in case of asset obsolescence or poor investment decisions.
Disadvantages	• Physical investments and financial investments are unrelated. • It can maintain the financial capital regardless of inappropriate investments or obsolescent assets. In competitive markets, this leads to a loss of market value in competitive markets.	• It requires complex formulation and yields results subject to different interpretations. • It entails greater costs in implementation (data validation and so on). • It increases the problem of information asymmetry for the regulator by increasing the technical complexity of regulation.

Source: Authors.

The two approaches require different indexes to express the asset value in real terms (that is, constant dollars). Under the financial investment approach, a general price index should be used, because it reflects the change in the purchasing power of money. Under the physical capital approach, the ideal choice would be an index (or a properly weighted combination of indexes) that reflects inasmuch as possible the changes in costs related to the purchase/installation/construction of the assets.

Table A7.1 summarizes the advantages and disadvantages of the different alternatives.

Once an approach is chosen, regulatory decisions on the return on capital, indexation, redundant assets, and other matters must be consistent with that approach.

Regulatory asset base and accounting

Privatizations introduce a break in the institutional scheme of the sector, which necessarily affects the way a firm's capital is reflected. The relation between the regulated asset base and the value of capital in the firm's financial statements will depend greatly on the treatment given to the initial capital value during the privatization process. This effect is only temporary. As time passes, the firm's financial statements reflect the investments carried out under the new rules, and the valuation at the time of privatization loses its relative weight. However, due to the typical long useful life of infrastructure assets, this transition may last for several decades.

The following sections review real cases of asset valuation in Argentina, the United Kingdom, Bolivia, and Chile and a case involving accounting assets in Mali.

Asset Valuation on the Basis of Best Bid Price: Argentina

The Argentine case concerns creation of a new company and valuation of the assets to be transferred based on the best bid price.

Argentina began its privatization process in 1991. A basic law governing the sector was passed by Congress in December 1991 and went into effect in January 1992. The main thermal plants and distribution and transmission companies owned by the national government were sold to the private sector through competitive bidding in 1992 and 1993, and most of the national government's hydro plants were sold the following year. Segba, the state-owned electricity company, was divided into seven companies: four generation companies and three distribution companies: Edenor, Edesur, and Edelap.

Valuation of the initial asset base was similar for Edenor and Edesur.[1] Each company's initial valuation (July 1992) was made by Banco Nacional de Desarrollo (Banade) on the basis of forecast cash flows and was considered the official budgeted value. This valuation was supposed to be the accounting valuation at the moment of privatization, and no mention was made of the price paid in the bidding process. However, decree 282/93 (February 1993) took into account the fact that the official value proposed by Banade was significantly below the price obtained in the bidding process, and thus it stated that assets were to be valued on the basis of the price paid in the bidding process. As a result, financial statements were calculated from scratch on a paid price basis—the price obtained in the bidding process—to reflect the true market value at the time.

Flotation of Shares on the Stock Market: United Kingdom

The UK case illustrates the sale of an existing company through flotation of its shares on the stock market. The new companies own the assets and operate under licences. The values that they paid were substantially lower than the adjusted historic values in the financial statements.

The issue of the valuation of existing assets was addressed in the water and gas industries. At privatization, this valuation was intended to ensure that existing owners would neither gain nor lose from the change in regime. Calculations of the "indicative value" required estimation of the cash flows that the existing assets would have generated if the regulatory regime had not changed. The discounted value of this cash flow is defined as the indicative value (IV):

$$IV = \sum_{t=1}^{T} \frac{zK_{t-1}+D_t}{(1+r)^t} = \frac{z}{r}K_0 + \frac{(r-z)}{r}\sum_{t=1}^{T} \frac{D_t}{(1+r)^t},$$

where K_{t-1} is the replacement cost value of assets at the end of period $t-1$, D_t is asset depreciation (current cost), r is cost of capital, z is the accounting rate of return on existing assets, and K_0 is the replacement cost at the end of period 0.

This complicated procedure was necessary because assets that were in the public sector had no observable market value before privatization. However, when prices were reset, some corrections were made to transform that value into an equivalent market value. For example, when reviewing the rate of return for the transportation assets of British Gas (BG), the Monopolies and Mergers Commission (MMC) stated that

> *Ofgas and BG agreed on the need to allow for the difference between the amounts realized from the sale of BG and BG's CCA [capital cost allowance] asset value at that time, and for subsequent discrepancies between the stock market's valuation and CCA-based values, referred to [...] as the market to assets ratio (MAR) [...] on balance a MAR of 60 percent would seem reasonable, allowing shareholders to retain many of the gains since privatization. This ratio is of course to be applied only to the return on existing assets; it does not affect the return on new investment. (MMC 1993)*

Although the company and the MMC argued about the values of the cost of capital and the market-to-assets ratio (MAR), the regulator accepted the methodology. By doing so, it basically implied that corrections were not to be made on the existing assets but on the allowed rate of return on those assets, so for these assets the allowed rate of return should be the cost of capital times the MAR:

$$z = r \times MAR.$$

Privatization through Capitalization: Bolivia

This example illustrates privatization through capitalization. The best tender in the bidding process represents the value to be capitalized in the company.

In 1994, Bolivia reformed its electricity sector with a new legal framework that privatized the sector. Under the new structure, the sector was unbundled into separate generation, transmission, and distribution activities to allow establishment of a competitive market in which supply is represented by generators, and demand by distribution companies and consumers. Distribution, transmission, and generation are private, but only distribution and transmission are regulated.

Bolivia is the first emerging market economy to attempt privatization of the electricity supply industry through the capitalization process. The process is aimed at transferring half of the ownership of the state-owned companies to individuals who would in turn develop pension funds and capital markets. The process ensures capitalization through timely investments of amounts equal to those contributed by private investors.

Bolivia offered the enterprises for sale by international tender. The successful bidder paid the agreed price not to the government but to the company, doubling its net worth. The best tender in the bidding process represented the value to be capitalized in the company. This value is associated with the following concepts:

- new replacement value,
- asset that best serves demand, and
- adaptation to demand.

The cash was used for investment in the sector, stimulating expansion and efficiency improvements, as well as job creation. Initially, the strategic investor and the government each held 50 percent stakes in the new company. The government immediately gave its share in equal parts to all adult Bolivians.[2]

A7

Asset base accounting based exclusively on net replacement value: Chile

This case illustrates an asset base accounting based exclusively on net replacement value—that is, with no relation to the capital invested in the company.

Electricity sector. Chile started its reform process in the late 1980s. The norms included regulation of production, transportation, distribution, concessions, easements, prices, facility quality and safety conditions, machinery and instruments, and relations of the companies with the state and the private sector. In preparation for privatization, Chile began separating the different productive stages of the electricity sector in 1981. Divestiture of Chilectra resulted in creation of one generation company (Chilgener) and two distribution companies (Chilquinta in Valparaiso and Chilectra in Santiago). Endesa was broken into five independent distribution companies, three generating complexes (Endesa, Pullinque, and Pilmaiquén), and three independent integrated systems (Edelnor in the north, and Edelaysen and Edelmag in the extreme south).

The state assumed that electricity generation was a potentially competitive market but considered distribution and transmission to be local and natural monopolies and, therefore, in need of regulation. It used four privatization mechanisms: (1) sale of small distribution and generation subsidiaries of Endesa through public bidding (Saesa and Frontel), (2) privatization of large-scale distribution and generation companies by auctioning blocks of shares on the stock exchange, (3) sale of shares to the public in small quantities ("popular capitalism"), and (4) divestiture of ownership in two distributors (Chilectra and Chilquinta) through repayment in shares of the reimbursable financial contributions clients make in order to access the network (start-up investment).

Consumers whose demand for power is less than 2 megawatts face regulated prices; consumers demanding more than 2 megawatts are free to negotiate prices, power, and energy directly with generators or distribution companies.

Water and sanitation sector. Until the 1980s, the statutory, regulatory, and operative responsibilities of the water sector were vested in a public autonomous entity called Sendos (National Sanitary Services). Sendos directly operated 11 of the 13 regions in the country and was responsible for regulating the two autonomous state-owned companies (EMOS in Santiago and ESVAL in Region V) as well as many minor private or municipal companies. The reform in the late 1980s turned the regional companies into corporations in which public entities own 100 percent of the shares.

The largest companies in the sector have been privatized in the last few years. The companies were sold in a variety of ways: a strategic partner bought a block of shares through a bidding process and subscribed to a certain number of shares under a capital increase decided before the bidding, 10 percent of shares were sold in the stock market, and 10 percent of shares were sold to workers. The state retained ownership of at least 35 percent of the shares.

Regulatory asset base. Tariffs for public services are based on a model efficient company (engineering economic model). The assets of the model efficient company, not those of the real company, are used. Therefore, the asset base is based exclusively on the new replacement value and has no relation to the capital invested by the company.

Accounting of assets: Mali

The way in which private participation is introduced (concession, licence, sale of assets, management contract) greatly affects representation of assets in the firm's accounting.

In some forms of private participation—typically concessions—different types of assets coexist: transferred assets that are owned by the state, assets directly funded by third parties (users), and assets owned by the company. Regulatory accounting must deal with these different types of ownership in a way that ensures adequate transparency as well as proper allocation of funds among the different "owners."

In this regard, the case of EDM in Mali is typical. In 2000, the state sold a majority stake in the electricity and water operator EDM to a private joint venture (owned by SAUR, the Bouygues group, and I.P.S.; the latter entity is owned by the Aga Khan Fund for Economic Development).

Among the assets listed in the balance sheet were assets belonging to the *domaine concédé* (conceded domain or state assets) and assets belonging to the *domaine privé* (private domain).

Among the liabilities, considered quasi-equity, were subsidies from the state and from international donors and third-party contributions.

The electricity concession contract defines the assets belonging to the conceded domain as "hydroelectric works with land and buildings," and "works, lines, production, transport and distribution installations essential to the service." So these assets do not belong to the company, and they have to be handed over to the state at the end of concession, but they are listed in the company's balance sheet. The concession fee paid by the company to the state represents a rent for these assets.

The assets belonging to the private domain are the other assets, and all assets that will be acquired by the company during the life of the concession.

A further accounting differentiation is introduced between assets that must be handed over to the state at the end of concession (if belonging to the private sector, they will be acquired by the state or the next operator) and assets that need to be renewed (when assets life ends before the end of the concession). All these categories of assets benefit from a specific accounting treatment.

A7

Public and private assets essential to regulatory work should be identified as assets belonging to the state and should not be part of the regulatory asset base. These assets will not be included in the regulatory asset base when determining tariffs.

Some "public" assets were and are financed in part by subsidies from the state or from international agencies. Users finance connection equipment, for which they are charged. Therefore, these assets belong to users and should be clearly identified as belonging to them. The inclusion or exclusion of these assets in the regulatory asset base is a regulatory decision.

Regardless of the criteria adopted for valuation of the regulatory asset base and representation of that base in the financial statements at the time of privatization, reconciliation of the regulatory asset base and the asset value in the financial statements is a key element of regulatory accounting. This reconciliation calls for explicit rules for determination and valuation of the regulated asset base and for the way in which the accounting reconciliation between this valuation and the valuation in the financial statements should be performed for regulatory purposes.

Notes

1. The valuation approach was different for Edelap but after two years it was changed to the approach followed for the other two distribution companies.

2. When all six sectors in the plan (telecommunications, electricity, oil and gas, railways, aviation, and parts of mining) were privatized as described, about $2 billion of shares had been distributed to Bolivian adults, and about $2 billion in new funds were available for investment by the now privatized companies.

Bibliography

Allen Consulting Group. 2003. "Principles for Determining Regulatory Depreciation Allowances." Note to the Independent Pricing and Regulatory Tribunal of
New South Wales, Melbourne, Australia. www.ipart.nsw.gov.au.

Arizu, Beatriz, Luiz Maurer, and Bernard Tenenbaum. 2004. "Pass Through of
Power Purchase Costs: Regulatory Challenges and International Practices."
Energy and Mining Sector Board Discussion Paper 10, Energy and Mining
Sector Board, World Bank, Washington, DC.

Baron, D.P., and R.B. Myerson. 1982. "Regulating a Monopolist with Unknown
Costs." *Econometrica* 50 (4): 911–30.

Barton, A.D. 1977. *Anatomy of Accounting*. 2nd ed. Brisbane, Australia: University
of Queensland Press.

Beesley, M.E., and S.C. Littlechild. 1989. "The Regulation of Privatized Monopolies in the United Kingdom." In *Regulators and the Market*, ed. C. Veljanovski.
London: Institute of Economic Affairs.

Berg, S., and J. Tschirhart. 1988. *Natural Monopoly Regulation: Principles and
Practice*. Cambridge, UK: Cambridge University Press.

Byatt, I.C.R. 1991. "Office of Water Services: Regulation of Water and Sewerage."
In *Regulators and the Market,* ed. C. Veljanovski. London: Institute of Economic
Affairs.

Carey, A., M. Cave, R. Duncan, G. Houston, and K. Langford. 1994. "Accounting
for Regulation in UK Utililties." University of Bath School of Management,
Centre for the Study of Regulated Industries, Bath, and Institute of Chartered
Accountants in England and Wales, London.

Coelli, T., A. Estache, S. Perelman, and L. Trujillo. 2003. *A Primer on Efficiency
Measurement for Utilities and Transport Regulators*. Washington, DC: World
Bank Institute.

Dufils, P., C. Lopater, and E. Guyomard. 2002. *Comptable 2003*. Mémento Pratique Francis Lefebvre. Paris: Editions Francis Lefebvre.

ESC (Essential Services Commission [Australia]). 2004a. "Electricity Industry Guideline No. 3: Regulatory Information Requirements." Essential Services Commission, Victoria, Australia. www.esc.vic.gov.au.

———. 2004b. "Electricity Industry Guideline No. 3: Templates for Regulatory Accounting Statements." Essential Services Commission, Victoria, Australia. www.esc.vic.gov.au..

Estache, A., and P. Burns. 1999a. "Information, Accounting, and the Regulation of Concessioned Infrastructure Monopolies." Policy Research Working Paper 2034, World Bank, Washington, DC.

———. 1999b. "Infrastructure Concessions, Information Flows, and Regulatory Risk." Viewpoint 203, Finance, Private Sector, and Infrastructure Network, World Bank Group, Washington, DC.

Estache, A., M. Rodriguez Pardina, J. M. Rodríguez, and G. Sember. 2002. "An Introduction to Financial and Economic Modeling for Utility Regulators." Policy Research Working Paper 3001, World Bank, Washington, DC.

Estache, A., Q. Wodon, and V. Foster. 2002. "Accounting for Poverty in Infrastructure Reform: Learning from Latin America's Experience." World Bank, Washington, DC.

Friedlob, G.T., and F. Plewa, Jr. 2000. *Financial and Business Statements*. 2nd ed. Hauppauge, NY: Barron's Educational Series.

Galetovic, A., and A.E. Bustos. 2004. "Monopoly Regulation, Chilean Style: The Efficient-Firm Standard in Theory and Practice." Working Paper 180, Center for Applied Economics, University of Chile, Santiago.

Garrison, R.H., and E.W. Noreen. 1994. *Managerial Accounting*. Burr Ridge, IL: Irwin/McGraw-Hill.

Goodman, L.S. 1998. *The Process of Ratemaking*. Vienna, VA: Public Utilities Reports, Inc.

Green, R.J., and M. Rodriguez Pardina. 1999. *Resetting Price Controls for Privatized Utilities: A Manual for Regulators*. Washington, DC: Economic Development Institute of the World Bank.

Grifell-Tatjé, E., and C.A. Knox Lovell. 2003. "The Managers vs. the Consultants." *The Scandinavian Journal of Economics* 105 (1): 119–38.

Grout, P.A. 1997. "The Cost of Capital and Asset Valuation." In *Regulatory Review 1997*, ed. P. Vass. Bath, UK: Centre for the Study of Regulated Industries, University of Bath School of Management.

Guasch, J.L. 2004. *Granting and Renegotiating Infrastructure Concessions: Doing It Right.* Washington, DC: World Bank.

Horngren, C.T., and G. Foster. 1987. *Cost Accounting: A Managerial Emphasis.* 6th ed. Upper Saddle River, NJ: Prentice Hall.

Info-Communications Development Authority of Singapore. 2001. "Accounting Separation Guidelines." Annex A, Info-Communications Development Authority of Singapore.

IPART (Independent Pricing and Regulatory Tribunal of New South Wales). 2001. "Proposed Accounting Separation Code of Practice for Regulated Electricity Businesses in New South Wales." Issue 2, Section 3.4, IPART, Sydney, Australia. www.ipart.nsw.gov.au.

Kerf, M. 2000. "Do State Holding Companies Facilitate Private Participation in the Water Sector? Evidence from Côte d'Ivoire, the Gambia, Guinea, and Senegal." Policy Research Working Paper 2513, World Bank, Washington, DC.

Kerf, M., and D. Geradin. 2000. "Post-Liberalization Challenges in Telecommunications: Balancing Antitrust and Sector-Specific Regulation—Tentative Lessons from the Experiences of the United States, New Zealand, Chile and Australia." *World Competition: Law and Economics Review* 23 (1): 27–77.

Laffont, J.J. 1999. "Translating Principles into Practice in Regulation Theory." Working Paper, Centro de Estudios Económicos para la Regulación, Buenos Aires, Argentina.

Laffont, J.J., and J. Tirole. 1994. *A Theory of Incentives in Procurement and Regulation.* Cambridge, MA: MIT Press.

Laudon, K.C., and J.P. Laudon. 1998. *Management Information Systems: New Approaches to Organization and Technology.* 5th ed. Upper Saddle River, NJ: Prentice Hall.

Loeb, M., and W.A. Magat. 1979. "A Decentralized Method for Utility Regulation." *Journal of Law and Economics* 22 (2): 399–404.

MMC (Monopolies and Mergers Commission). 1993. *Gas and British Gas plc: Reports under the Gas and Fair Trading Acts.* London: HMSO.

———. 1997. *Northern Ireland Electricity plc.* London: HMSO.

Munasinghe, M. 1990a. *Electric Power Economics*. London: Butterworth-Heinemann Press.

———. 1990b. *Energy Analysis and Policy*. London: Butterworth-Heinemann Press.

NER (National Energy Regulator). 2002. "Regulatory Framework for the Economic Regulation of the Electricity Supply Industry of South Africa: A Discussion Document." Pricing and Tariff Department, NER, Pretoria, South Africa. www.ner.org.za.

OECD (Organisation for Economic Co-operation and Development). 1995. *Transfer Pricing Guidelines for Multinational Enterprises and Tax Administrations*. Paris: OECD.

OFFER (UK Office of Electricity Regulation). 1994. *Regional Electric Companies Price Review*. Birmingham, UK: OFFER.

Ofgem (Office of Gas and Electricity Markets). 2002. "The National Grid Company plc Regulatory Accounting Guidelines Working Paper." Ofgem, London.

Ofgem Chief Executive; Director General of Telecommunications; Director General of Water Services; Director General of Electricity and Gas Supply, Northern Ireland; Rail Regulator; Civil Aviation Authority; and Postal Services Commission. 2001. "The Role of Regulatory Accounts in Regulated Industries." Ofgem, London.

Ofwat (Office of Water Services). 1992. "Regulatory Accounting Guideline 1.03." Ofwat, London. www.ofwat.gov.uk.

———. 2002a. "Regulatory Accounting Guideline 3.05." Ofwat, London. www.ofwat.gov.uk.

———. 2002b. "The Review of Regulatory Accounting Guidelines: A Second Consultation Paper." Ofwat, London. www.ofwat.gov.uk.

———. 2003a. "Regulatory Accounting Guideline 1.03, 2.03, 3.05, 4.02 and 5.03." Ofwat, London. www.ofwat.gov.uk.

———. 2003b. "Regulatory Accounting Guideline 1.03: Guideline for Accounting of Current Costs and Regulatory Capital Values." Ofwat, London. www.ofwat.gov.uk.

Oxera. 2003. "Assessing Profitability in Competition Policy Analysis." Economic Discussion Paper 6. Prepared for the UK Office of Fair Trading, London.

Pintaux, P. 2002. "Le Système Comptable Ouest Africain (SYSCOA): L'intégration économique par la comptabilité." Tertiaire 104. Paris.

QCA (Queensland Competition Authority). 2003. "Electricity Distribution: Regulatory Accounting and Information Guidelines." August draft, QCA, Brisbane, Australia.

Rossi, M., and C. Ruzzier. 2001. "On the Regulatory Applications of Efficiency Measures." *Utilities Policy* 9 (2): 81–92.

Rosso, D.J., and C.S. Dorgan. 2002. "Arbitration and Dispute Resolution in the Electricity Industry." *Power Economics* 6 (6): 24–27.

Shim, J.K., and J.G. Siegel. 2000. *Modern Cost Management and Analysis.* 2nd ed. New York: Barron's Business Library.

Smith, W. 1997. "Utility Regulators—Decision-making Structures, Resources, and Start-up Strategy." *Viewpoint* 129, Finance, Private Sector and Infrastructure Network, World Bank, Washington, DC.

UEMOA (Union Economique et Monétaire Ouest Africaine). 1997. *Système Comptable Ouest Africain: guide d'application.* Paris: Foucher.

U.S. Financial Accounting Standards Board. 1978. "Statement of Financial Accounting Concepts No. 1." Norwalk, CT.

Utility Regulators Forum. "National Regulatory Reporting for Electricity Distribution and Retailing Businesses." Discussion paper. Australian Competition and Consumer Commission, Melbourne, Australia.

Walton, P. 2001. *La comptabilité anglo-saxonne.* Paris: La Découverte.

World Bank. 1996. "Water and Wastewater Utilities—Indicators." 2nd ed. Water and Sanitation Division, World Bank, Washington, DC.

———. 2002. "Financial Modeling of Regulatory Policy: Introduction to Theory and Practice." CD-ROM, World Bank Institute, Washington, DC.

Index

ECO-AUDIT
Environmental Benefits Statement

The World Bank is committed to preserving endangered forests and natural resources. The Office of the Publisher has chosen to print *Accounting for Infrastructure Regulation: An Introduction* on recycled paper with 30 percent post-consumer waste, in accordance with the recommended standards for paper usage set by the Green Press Initiative, a nonprofit program supporting publishers in using fiber that is not sourced from endangered forests. For more information, visit www.greenpressinitiative.org.

Saved:

- 7 trees
- 318 lbs. of solid waste
- 2,478 gallons of waste water
- 597 lbs. of net greenhouse gases
- 5 million BTUs of total energy

green
press
INITIATIVE

www.ingramcontent.com/pod-product-compliance
Lightning Source LLC
Chambersburg PA
CBHW080530220326
41599CB00032B/6264